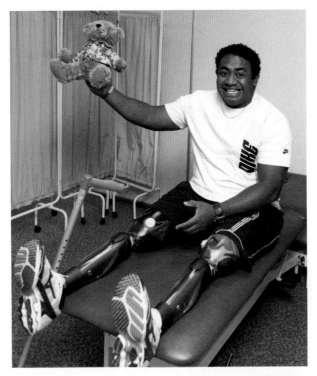

Private Derek Derenalagi, 2nd Battalion, The Mercian Regiment

The Hero Inside

PHOTOGRAPHS BY GILL SHAW

Quiller

IN SUPPORT OF
HELP *for* HEROES

IN SUPPORT OF

HELP *for* HEROES

CHARITY NO
1120920

The Hero Inside
PHOTOGRAPHS *BY* GILL SHAW

Quiller

Today the word 'hero' is too often used; for me it is a very special word and should be used sparingly: a hero is someone distinguished by exceptional courage, nobility and fortitude. This wonderful book by Gill Shaw is to raise funds for just such men and women injured in the line of duty whilst serving our country – **real** heroes.

For me, meeting The Royal Anglian Regiment changed my life significantly. From that first day at Elizabeth Barracks, Pirbright, it was clear that I was amongst dedicated, courageous, disciplined men and women and what's more they were all young – well nearly all!

We often talk of the veterans of past wars and conflicts; perhaps we had the chance to speak with our fathers, mothers, grandfathers, and grandmothers who served our country in the past, we listened closely to their tales of war, hardship, bravery and determination. The young men and women serving today far from home are the same people, the young Platoon Commander who landed on the beaches of Normandy 65 years ago and the young Platoon Commander serving in Helmand Province, Afghanistan. Divided only by the years, nothing more.

Since becoming a Patron of **Help for Heroes** I have had the privilege and honour of meeting many young servicemen and women who have been wounded. Without exception they are proud and they are humble, and above all, they do not consider themselves to be heroes; we know differently.

With the **Help for Heroes** team, Bryn and Emma Parry have highlighted the help that so many servicemen and women need but never ask for.

I can only hope that what Gill has done is to bring together a book that will hopefully inspire you 'to do your bit' in helping these servicemen and women who have already given so much for our country and us.

I am incredibly proud and honoured to be a Patron of this wonderful charity. I hope that by supporting our Armed Services and in particular the many wounded young men and women, you are proud of yourself – you should be.

Thank you.

Ross Kemp

I am Sgt Mark Sutcliffe of the 2nd Battalion The Royal Anglian Regiment – 'The Poachers'.

On 18 July 2006, I was on a foot patrol whilst deployed on OP TELIC 8. We came under enemy fire and an RPG (rocket propelled grenade) was fired which directly hit my left leg – unfortunately taking it clean off. The subsequent bleeding was massive. My multiple Commander attempted to stem the bleeding stump, himself now covered in my blood, and applied life-saving first aid, whilst one of the other lads was trying to reassure me. I will always be so grateful to the guys that helped me.

I was then placed into the back of a Warrior

Fighting Vehicle crewed by soldiers of The Light Infantry, now 5 Rifles. One of the other lads found what was left of my leg and placed it in the back of the wagon.

At the speed of a thousand gazelles, I was evacuated to the Shatt al-Arab hotel and was immediately set upon by lots of medics and the doctor. I was swiftly whisked away by the MERT to the Field Hospital at Shaibah Logistics Base. From there on, it all went slightly blurry due to the morphine. Next thing I knew, I woke up in Intensive Care.

After a few days I was aero-meded back to Selly Oak Hospital in Birmingham, where I spent the best part of four months recovering. My family and friends provided me with so much support; I don't think I could have got through it without them.

I was then transferred to DMRC Headley Court, where I learnt to walk again with the aid of a prosthetic leg. The comradeship at Headley Court was excellent and, because most of us were missing a limb or in some cases lots of limbs, the banter was good – comparing wounds with true squaddie humour! I was an in-patient at Headley Court for just over three months and then I was discharged, having an excellent level of mobility.

Having been on sick leave for a while, it was time to think about getting back to work. My battalion were in the process of moving to Germany, so I asked if I could become a Military Liaison Officer at Selly Oak Hospital – the idea being that I could give something back.

After a few months I was in Birmingham learning the ropes. We as MLOs are responsible 24/7 for providing the vital link between deployed formations, unit rear parties to the military casualties. In addition we assist Casualty Visiting Officers with their plan of action when escorting families to Selly Oak Hospital. When appropriate we organise patient outings therefore allowing the injured soldiers a degree of normalisation. It's possibly the most rewarding job I have ever done and I continue to be there till the present day. ∎

On duty in Iraq, 2005

I am an ex-Royal Engineer and now work for BAE Systems working with British and other Armed Forces personnel.

By the grace of God I went through my military career uninjured, and I just think anyone that does get injured now deserves the very best help they can get, and that is why I feel very strongly about supporting **Help for Heroes**.

At a stopover on my bike ride on the outskirts of Birmingham, outside Selly Oak Hospital, feeling very hot and bothered I was lucky enough to be cooled down by three nurses! ▮

As military nurses, we are aware of the trauma servicemen sometimes go through. Alongside our NHS colleagues, we continue to look after our sick and wounded soldiers, providing the best possible care.

Princess Mary's RAF Nursing Services
From left: Corporals Christine Bratten, Steph Ross and Helen Owens.

I served as a Platoon Commander in 12 Brigade Reconnaissance Force on Operation HERRICK 6, Afghanistan 2007. On 26 April 2007 during an operation in the Sangin Valley, I was wounded in action by a rocket propelled grenade after having moved forward and extracted one of my platoon members who had been shot and wounded. I sustained severe fragmentation wounds to both arms and legs and was evacuated back, along with the other casualty, to a helicopter landing site (HLS). Throughout this process the vehicle that was being used to conduct the CASEVAC was under sustained and heavy enemy fire, whilst the remainder of the Force, severely outnumbered, were fiercely engaged in close combat. The first HLS was untenable due to accurate and heavy indirect enemy fire, forcing the helicopter to overshoot and make another approach to a different site. The second site was still under fire, but less so. We were extracted by Chinook helicopter back to the field hospital at Camp Bastion. After undergoing surgery to stabilise us, we spent a further four days in the hospital before being repatriated to the UK. I was admitted to Selly Oak Hospital for more surgery and treatment before eventually arriving at the Defence Medical Rehabilitation Centre, Headley Court.

During the four months at DMRC Headley Court, I had to learn how to walk again and use my arms due to the nerve damage sustained. My only goal was to return to my platoon by September. This was contrary to the medical prognosis that deemed the ability to run would not come before Christmas 2007. In the second week of September, having completed the required fitness assessments and, despite being partially paralysed in my right hand and foot, I was discharged from Headley Court to 'Return To

Unit, Camp Bastion' for the remainder of the tour. Unfortunately, just before boarding the flight, I was removed from the manifest and remained in the UK until the Unit returned and disbanded.

In March 2008 I completed the Bataan Memorial Death March in New Mexico, USA in aid of **Help for Heroes**. In December 2008, although partially paralysed in my hand and foot and still receiving treatment, I was upgraded to full fitness and I continue to serve in the Army.

As an Old Reedonian I was more than delighted when Peter Thomason asked Lieutenant Mike Foster Van Der Elst of the Rifles, also an Old Reedonian, and myself to support Reed's School to raise money for **Help for Heroes** and describe our experiences of contemporary operations to the pupils. ◼

On a personal note, the initial desire to organise this event and to motivate others in the school to take part was born, not from any grand moment of personal loss or human contact with a veteran, but from something some would consider rather more mediocre, from simply watching television. I saw on the news one night a piece on the wounded returning from Afghanistan and Iraq and found myself stunned by the realisation that the returning injured soldiers were not all aged veterans, but in fact many were no older than

'**I am delighted that the students became so passionate about this particular cause.**'

David Jarrett – Headmaster of
Reed's School, Cobham

myself, and now they found themselves burdened with terrible injuries as a reward for the immense bravery of their youth.

This initial shock would only be compounded when, a few weeks later, I had the honour to listen to a speech from an old boy of the school, Captain Michael Holgate, who himself was wounded in combat and had been rehabilitated at Headley Court. He was full of praise for the institution. To say that I was inspired would be an understatement and, from the very next day, I began trying to persuade other sixth formers and the school's Senior Management Team to support me in a bid to raise money for **Help for Heroes** and for people like Captain Holgate and Major Phil Packer, who deserve no less.

I was in the fortunate position of belonging to a school with both the facilities and charitable spirit to make such a day possible and the support of all the children, parents and staff was quite overwhelming. It just goes to show that **Help for Heroes** is a charity with a cause that every age group cares greatly about, and rightly so. I truly believe that, no matter what one's opinion about the virtues of war, or indeed Britain's military involvement in the Middle East, if any one of us found ourselves surrounded by the sand, the heat, the bullets and the bombs of those conflicts, we would take immense comfort in knowing that millions of people back home supported charities such as **Help for Heroes**. For this reason I think that its worthiness as a cause is indisputable. ■

From left: Alex Stead, Daniel Allpress, Peter Thomason, Captain Mike Holgate, Headmaster David Jarrett, Lieutenant Mike Foster Van Der Elst, William Soloman, Charlie Kerr, Baite Beyai.

I own a small garden design company called All Seasons Design and, in 2008, I approached **Help for Heroes** with a wonderful idea for a Sanctuary Garden that could be built at Chelsea Flower Show, so raising awareness and money. Having gained their blessing to represent **Help for Heroes** in this manner, I then put the design forward to the selection board at the Royal Horticultural Society. Two long months later, in December, we were informed that we had gained one of the few places for an Urban Garden.

Time then seemed to speed up with the necessary organisation, the finding of a sponsor, the planning, the sourcing of materials and plants and finally the construction of the garden itself at the most important garden show there is, not just in Britain, but worldwide. Thanks to a multitude of wonderful and hardworking people, we were awarded a Silver Medal, which was a moment I will remember for a long time to come. We did what we set out to do, in that we raised awareness of the work of **Help for Heroes** to a cross-section of people who might not have heard of them, we again raised their profile in the

national newspapers and we raised much needed funding for their ongoing projects. A big pat on the back to all involved.

But you may want to know why I set out to design and build this garden in the first place. I have been involved with **Help for Heroes** since the charity was first created, initially because they were raising funds for the Joint Service Rehabilitation Unit at Headley Court. I have always felt that I needed to give something back to Headley Court, where I learnt to use my legs again after a climbing accident, several years ago, had left me with a broken back, legs and pelvis. Once I had become involved with **Help for Heroes**, what is there to disagree with? Raising money for **Help for Heroes** is my way of doing my bit to help our wounded servicemen, one of whom, one day, may be my husband.

The idea for the garden itself did not come in a blinding flash of light, but was the rather slow development of an idea when my husband (a Battery Commander with the Royal Artillery) announced he was returning to operations in Afghanistan. I wished to create a sanctuary for those who do not return safely, somewhere where they can find focus and peace to deal with either their physical or mental injuries after the ordeal of operations. This idea grew further after talking with other Army wives who felt as I do. This was about taking an active involvement in caring for our husbands, wives, boyfriends, girlfriends, sons and daughters. That which happens to them is obviously beyond our control, but we are doing all we can to ensure that, when they return to us, if they are injured, they have the best care possible.

Ours was a garden built for heroes, by heroes, to raise awareness and funding for **Help for Heroes**.

‘It was a treat to come across the Help for Heroes garden when I visited the Chelsea Flower Show. I liked very much its quiet intensity, and it was the perfect atmosphere for contemplating just how much is done for us by our Armed Forces, and what terrible sacrifices they continue to make for their country. ’

Jane Asher

Non-political, nor critical, the aim of **Help for Heroes** is simple and straightforward: to help those who have been wounded on current operations.

Over the past eighteen months, I have had the honour and privilege to see at first hand both the genesis of the idea behind **Help for Heroes**, and the effect that it has had on the welfare of our wounded servicemen and women. The entire experience has been both inspiring and humbling. What Bryn Parry and his team have achieved in financial terms is beyond any of our most optimistic expectations, but this success is about much more than the money raised, important though that is.

Our soldiers on operations would never call themselves heroes – they see themselves as ordinary people doing an ordinary job. I would contend that anyone who joins the Forces knowing that they may be called upon to make the ultimate sacrifice in service of their country is indeed a hero. What **Help for Heroes** has achieved, as well as the launch of exciting projects such as the new pool at Headley Court, is to ensure that our young men and women who return from operations, having suffered appalling and life-changing injuries, never feel that their sacrifice is taken for granted by the people of the United Kingdom.

Furthermore, through fresh and novel fund-raising and publicity strategies, the people of this country have been provided a means by which they can show their support and backing for their Armed Forces, ensuring that our soldiers, sailors and airmen occupy a place in the nation's heart for many years to come.

I know that I speak on behalf of all ranks in the Army – as well as their families – when I thank **Help for Heroes** for all these magnificent achievements. We are all deeply grateful. ■

> ❝ I would contend that anyone who joins the Forces knowing that they may be called upon to make the ultimate sacrifice in service of their country is indeed a hero. ❞

'Help for Heroes shouldn't be needed – but it is. I have seen mates from the Army come through hell after serious injuries and then come out smiling thanks to some of the fantastic care we've had in place in the past, but, as you know, a lot of this has gone now; for example the dedicated military hospitals. I admire the courage of the men and women serving Britain in the Armed Forces now; they do the job with poor pay and poor equipment, but always come out on top. They are truly inspirational and thank goodness for Help for Heroes. '

Pete Bray is a former SAS Sergeant who left the Army at the age of 40 to go around the world (well the cold parts), in a kayak. (He was a boat specialist with the SAS and fond of these little boats that you paddle!) He became the only person to kayak, solo and unsupported, across the North Atlantic in 1991 and in the summer of 2009, at the tender age of 53, he set his sights on raising money for **Help for Heroes** by rowing solo and unsupported across the North Atlantic. ■

I am a Lieutenant in the 1st The Queen's Dragoon Guards (QDG).

A short time after a 'festive' Christmas, well as festive as you can expect in Afghanistan, and a very quiet New Year in Musa Qaleh, we were tasked to move to a new location south of our current base. The troop had high morale and was generally excited, although anxious, about the task we had to do. We knew we were going to be there for a little while, so filled as much 'real' food into our vehicles as we could. Unfortunately there were many other more important items that all needed to go, so only a few packets of Haribo made it to the Patrol Base!

As is often the case, moving in vehicles is a very dangerous and often time-consuming task, checking and clearing, marking, identifying IEDs (Improvised Explosive Devices) and mines. During the festive season it had rained, much like home

With Captain Dale Walker, Army physio at Headley Court

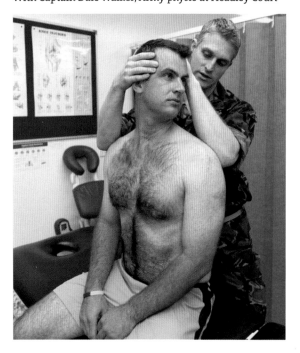

(not the only thing like home – the Christmas lunch even included brussel sprouts), and rain it did. Afghanistan being a very dry country with a lot of desert doesn't cope so well with rain, especially not lots of rain. The day of our move proved exciting, as we had more to consider than the usual threat of IEDs; the weather had turned the tracks we use into muddy swamps which wasn't good, we couldn't see our tracks nor could we see any possible ground disturbances, a tell-tale sign of suspicious activity.

After some delay we arrived late on the afternoon of New Year's Day. The Regiment we were taking over from had given us the brief of what to expect and we merrily settled into our new 'home'. It wasn't long before we had aroused the suspicion of the enemy (there was a good chance they'd watched us move in). We knew from our interpreters that the Taliban was in the area and they were likely to 'have a go' at some point over the next few days.

About five hours into our stay, the first shots were fired and we were in 'contact' in our new home. Fortunately the contact was short-lived, almost like the enemy were giving us a bit of a trial to see how good we were!

Early on 2 January 2009, as I was eating a ration pack of bacon and beans, the first of what was to be a six-hour contact began. The sentries on the roof alerted all members of the troop to their predisposed positions. By all accounts, it was the fastest I've ever eaten a ration pack! My role was to back up the Troop Leader in Command of PB Yubraj. Whilst he was coordinating the air assets and mortars and relaying the information to the Officer Commanding in another base 600m away, I was relaying the relevant information to the guys on the ground and on the roof alongside me.

> **The Medics at Patrol Base Yubraj saved my life. I had lost a great deal of blood, my lung had collapsed and my windpipe had been severed.**

After twenty minutes or so, the intensity of the fire fight increased rapidly. We started to receive RPGs (Rocket Propelled Grenades) over our heads and some were falling just short of our position. With the rate of fire increasing, the noise levels were enormous and it was one large 'bang' that was to result in my early return home.

I and another two members of C Sqn QDG had been struck by an 'air burst' RPG. This was a fluke shot – if an RPG doesn't hit its target, occasionally it self-destructs in the air. Unfortunately for us, our RPG exploded two metres or so above our heads, covering the rooftop with metal shrapnel. I received a 2p-sized piece of shrapnel in the centre of my neck just below my Adam's apple. I realised I had been injured immediately, as the shrapnel had struck a main artery and began to bleed considerably. I was very quickly taken off the rooftop where I was attended to by our female Corporal Medic and her team. At this point, the other two casualities were also being treated for their wounds and the task was now to return us to Camp Bastion for further medical treatment.

The Medics at Patrol Base Yubraj saved my life. I had lost a great deal of blood, my lung had collapsed and my windpipe had been severed. The Corporal Medic prepared the other two casualties and myself for evacuation via RAF Chinook to Camp Bastion. The contact was still ongoing so we had to be moved to a safe area away from the fighting in order for the Chinook of 18 Squadron to pick us up. They arrived in incredible time to return us to Camp Bastion, where we were operated on.

I returned to the UK in the back of an RAF C17 Transport Aircraft. I was placed in an induced coma to fly me home. I arrived on 3 January 2009, only 20 hours after I had been injured, at Selly Oak Hospital, Birmingham.

I spent a further three weeks in hospital, two of those in a coma in Intensive Care and one on the Military Ward. I returned home after that and was told to rest. At this point it became apparent that I required another operation to repair the artery that had been severed, as my arm wasn't working as well as it should.

After many visits to hospital and time spent at the Defence Medical Rehabilitation Centre, Headley Court, I underwent my second operation which has been a great success. The other two casualties injured with me on 2 January have returned to work already.

Throughout the course of my injuries, the medical attention I have received has been excellent. I am looking forward to returning to work in Germany later this year where I can carry out the job I have trained to do! ■

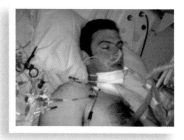

Selly Oak Hospital, January 2009

Marine Ben McBean (right) with Mark Elliott (far left), Chief of Staff at **Help for Heroes**.

On 28 February 2008, when I was based at Kajaki in Afghanistan, we went out for a normal everyday foot patrol. It was the first hot day in about a month and I was getting really frustrated because the flies were landing on my sweaty forehead. After a long one-hour walk, we arrived at the compound we were going to clear. We had to run across 50–60 metres of open ground to get there. Go, go, go and off we went. I was running as fast as I could, following the guy in front and, before I knew it, I was upside down and my face was burning. My leg was stood up on the ground below and, before I had time to click on to what had happened, I hit the deck. Sitting up, I noticed my leg was missing. My arm was broken and facing the wrong way four times over. My right arm had a hole in it, my testicle was hanging out and my other leg was in bits. Ouch. First thing on my mind was 'Get someone to take a photo', so I did. I then woke up in the UK to find my arm was missing. Gutted. This year, I decided to run the London Marathon, which I finished in 6 hours 15 minutes. My doctors told me not to even think about it but there was no way that was going to stop me! My prosthetic leg cut into my stump, making it swell to twice its size. I was fine, actually, until 13 miles when I changed my dressing. When I pushed it back on, the pain was unbearable. I couldn't even lift my head, but it would have been too embarrassing to stop. So many people were supporting me and I kept thinking of my mates serving in Afghanistan on the front line and that's what kept me going. ◼

The idea came during a break for lunch at a driven shoot in Hampshire. The three of us co-organisers, Andrew Lally, Shaun Miller and I, were discussing how we could raise money for this fantastic cause.

I have a step-brother who is serving as a Combat Medic in Afghanistan and I don't think people fully appreciate the danger these young men and women face every day. By all accounts their living conditions are far from ideal as well!

Whilst we can't do anything about what is happening so far away, the specialised rehabilitation of our war wounded is an absolute priority and **Help for Heroes** is actively concerned in making this happen.

The following letter was received from Stephen Murray, project manager for the new Purdey Sporter Gun, after our shoot:

'We were delighted to support **Help for Heroes** *by raising a couple of teams of Purdey Gunmakers to take part in this shoot. We all recognise* **Help for Heroes** *as a really worthwhile cause, assisting as it does the recuperation of servicemen and women injured in action, and which reminds us all of the debt of gratitude we owe to our Armed Forces.'*

We are honoured to have been involved and hope to be able to contribute more next year and in the years to come. ◼

Lee Henderson **Bewl Barrel Half-Marathon**

My name is Lee Henderson and I am a company director. My father died of motor neurone disease and, with that in mind, a few years ago I decided to start raising funds for those with that horrible disease.

Whilst doing various things, like climbing Snowdon in a suit of armour and reaching the summit of Mera Peak in Nepal in 2008 (22,000ft), I created 'The Bewl Barrel Race' as a local challenge and to raise funds for charities. Basically this is a pretty tough team half-marathon, run with a full 55-kilogram beer barrel (though you can run with an empty one, as an option!). The idea is that each year the winner of the race may choose which charity to raise funds for next time.

Captain Dominic Crisp from The Royal Marines helped us launch The Bewl Barrel Race in November 2007, but he unfortunately lost his life early last year in a climbing accident.

My team won the last event and **Help for Heroes** was chosen for several reasons. Firstly, in memory of Dom Crisp, after whom the trophy is named. Secondly, because many of my family are, or were, in the Forces and lastly because I lost a cousin in the first Gulf War.

I feel that any funds raised show some appreciation of what these young people are doing for us. ■

Top right: Nathan Massini, Adam Payne, Will Finden, Tommy Massini, Keith McCormack, Graham Payne, Richard Heath, James Cockerill, Tom How.

Centre right: Simon Jordan, Lee Henderson, Dave Elliott, Brian Anderson, Paul Miles, Chris Finan.

Below right: Claire Mans, Jo Crisp, Katy Woolley, Johnny Porter, Sarah Downes, Louisa Rogerson.

'Which is the fit one?! I have run a few marathons in my short life but the 2009 London Marathon will go down as the very best! No, it was not my fastest time but to have the privilege and honour to run with Marine Ben McBean, and on the same course as John Sandford-Hart and Major Phil Packer, was simply incredible. We often talk about heroes; I can say with hand on heart that on the 26 April 2009, I ran with my heroes... All real heroes. '

John Sandford-Hart

I am a former member of the Royal Electrical and Mechanical Engineers. My Ringwood-based company – Signworks – carries out work for The Rifles Regiment.

Seven years ago, I lost a leg in a powerboat accident when another boat crashed into me whilst I was racing off Cornwall. Thirteen painful operations failed to restore my mobility, so I decided to have my leg amputated. It's too early to say for sure, but it seems like it was the right decision.

I agreed to take part in this year's London Marathon after receiving a phone call from an Army friend whilst recovering in hospital. I was full of drugs at the time and so I said Yes! I was the last one in and completed this gruelling task in 11 hours on one leg and crutches.

I hold two Guinness Records now, one was for the fastest man on two legs and crutches, and now I hold the one for the fastest man on one leg and crutches!

Help for Heroes has always been close to my heart, as my Dad served a lifetime in the RAF.

Richard Glover and I wanted to do something really spectacular to honour our Armed Forces.

It was a case of mind over matter. We wanted to show people that, if we could do it, anyone can.

My next challenge in 2009 is to climb Kilimanjaro. ■

Left to right: John Sandford-Hart, Mark Elliott and Marine Ben McBean.

Lance Corporal Jonathon Le Galloudec RIFLES

On 7 May 2007, I deployed to Iraq.

One month later, on 7 June 2007, late at night, I was shot in the spine by an insurgent sniper.

I was lying on the ground, unable to move, paralysed from the waist down,

Two mates came to rescue me. Between them they both dragged me about 40 yards and then we all got shot. One of them was shot in the arm; the other was fatally wounded and died next to me.

The one who got shot in the arm managed to get away to cover.

Twenty-five minutes later, a rescue party finally got to me and evacuated me to Basra Field Hospital, where I underwent a six-hour operation to remove the bullet.

When I woke up, I was told I was paralysed from the waist down.

I was then moved to Selly Oak Hospital, where they said I would never walk again.

However, exactly three months later, I was able to walk out of the hospital.

Learning to walk again was the hardest thing I have ever had to do in my whole life.

Coming back from the brink of death and getting back to full-time employment with the same Battalion that I started with, is an achievement. ▨

I joined the Army in 2001 and, whilst serving in the Royal Army Medical Corps, I completed tours to Iraq, Bosnia and Afghanistan.

On 6 September 2006, in Helmand Province, Afghanistan, I was involved in a mine strike incident that seriously injured me and a number of other soldiers whom I was deployed to support.

I suffered a collapsed lung and extensive shrapnel wounds.

Since my recovery, I have been able to continue service and I have successfully applied for a place on the Commissioning Course at the Royal Military Academy Sandhurst. ■

'It shows a lot about the man that, despite picking up a serious injury whilst on patrol in Afghanistan, Officer Cadet Alex Craig has continued with his life in the Army and, indeed, has decided to try and progress his career by coming to the Royal Military Academy Sandhurst.

His enthusiasm, commitment and courage, both physical and mental, mean that he is a pleasure to teach. I have no doubt he will go on to lead his soldiers extremely well in the tough challenges that lie ahead and I wish him all the best!'
Captain Rob Moseley RTR,
12 Platoon Commander RMAS

'Since joining the Army seven years ago, Officer Cadet Craig has had a good career in the Royal Army Medical Corps but he has decided to try and better himself and his career by becoming an officer.

He is making the transition from soldier very well and is proving himself to be a very capable Officer Cadet. I am sure he will have a good future career in whichever regiment he decides to join.'
CSgt Ryan Bowness Yorks,
12 Platoon RMAS

Helmand Province, Afghanistan, August 2006

I was injured in Afghanistan in 2006 following an RPG attack. I received numerous injuries to my upper and lower limbs that resulted in me breaking all the bones in my legs and losing function in my right hand due to nerve damage.

Despite these injuries, I now dedicate my time to raising money and awareness for military charities. In 2008 I did the **Help for Heroes** Big Battlefield Bike Ride, a 360-mile ride through France on an adapted bike. In 2009, I completed the London Marathon, and am doing the UK 24-hour 3 Peak Challenge and also a tandem skydive with the Red Devils.

People I find inspiring are people such as Bear Grylls and Lance Armstrong and athletes who have overcome illness and serious injuries, who then go on and achieve amazing things. It shows how determination can help you overcome anything. It was hearing inspiring stories like theirs, and also being surrounded by people at Headley Court, who had far worse injuries than mine yet were still determined to crack on, that really helped me get through the times when I was feeling a bit sorry for myself. They made me realise that I was only going to get out of life what I put into it. ■

Top, wearing glasses – Barry Clarke, left – Brian Rowley, right – son Daniel Rowley 'the brains', bottom – Anthony Rowley (cousin of Brian).

Anthony Rowley, Barry Clarke, Brian and Daniel Rowley **The Welsh 3000s Challenge**

There are four members of the walking team and two of us, Barry Clarke and myself, have between us worked in the MoD for over 40 years. This has involved working with members of the 'Green Machine' and Royal Marines to ensure that the material they needed was purchased and supplied.

Seeing our wounded returning from operational theatres and to realise that they could be guys, friends even, that we had worked with, was shocking. I always wonder if I could have done anything different in my job to have made a difference at the sharp end in Iraq or 'Stan.

It can be humbling to hear of their fortitude in the face of the injuries they have suffered and then disappointing to hear colleagues complain that 'the office is too cold'.

I broached the subject of doing something for **Help for Heroes** to the other members of the walking team and was elated at their wish to crack on and get it sorted.

I know it is a cliché, but the walk is our way of showing that our Armed Forces have now, and always will have, our support and gratitude. ▮

I am WO2 Andy Newell. I am a serving Sergeant Major in the Parachute Regiment and currently work in MOD Abbey Wood. When I was injured in Afghanistan on 26 July 2006 I was the Operations Warrant Officer of the Pathfinders (PF), the Advance Force for 16 Air Assault Brigade based in Colchester.

At the time of the injury I was leading a relief convoy from Camp Bastion to Musa Qaleh. After plenty of contact with the Taliban on the way, we finally arrived in the town square to be greeted by friendly Afghan National Police and some Royal Engineers, flown in to reinforce the PF lads. I said I would just check that the compound gates were open, before getting everyone safely inside. Suddenly I found myself lying face down on the floor with my right arm underneath my body. After a few seconds I tried to move my arm, but only the top half moved while the bottom half stayed put, causing me a lot of pain. I thought I had been shot by a sniper so I lay still just in case I was still in his sights! No one came to sort me out so after a while I stood up and walked into the compound. I was starting to get dizzy by now through loss of blood, so I said to the medic, 'I need to see the doc pretty urgently'. He asked me why so I said 'because I've been shot, you nugget!'

A passing US Blackhawk flew me back to Camp Bastion. After surgery I woke to discover from X-rays that the bone in my arm had been shattered into more than 60 pieces. I was told that the only reason my arm hadn't been amputated was that the bullet hadn't hit an artery! I was a very lucky man. Two days later I had more surgery and was then flown back to the UK and admitted to Selly Oak Hospital in Birmingham.

The next day, just as I was being wheeled down for another operation, a nurse said my wife was on her way. We hadn't seen each other for over five months, and I was quite concerned how she would react, seeing me with a beard and still smelling to high heaven as I hadn't had a chance to have a proper shower. As she rounded the corner, I was struck by how beautiful she looked with her long blonde hair swirling about her as she rushed towards me, a big smile on her face. Suddenly she slowed down and uttered the immortal line 'and that bloody beard can come off', which made us both laugh out loud! I instantly knew that she would be ok with everything.

From Selly Oak I went to the DMRC at Headley Court, an awesome facility. To date I have been admitted to the 'Upper Limbs Group' there a total of nine times. When I first went there I was unable to use my arm or hand at all but have since learned how to write again and have regained some functionality in my arm and shoulder. I have had several operations, including three humeral nail insertions and two bone grafts.

Despite all the pain and discomfort, the setback to my career and the effect on relationships, still I battle on because that is what we do in the military. We just get on with it.

I have met so many inspirational people along the way, like Simon Weston, the Falklands hero, and Chris Holmes, a blind Paralympian who has won nine gold medals for swimming. Then there are all those at **Help for Heroes** who dedicate hours and hours of their time to raising money for us, and also the members of 'Toe in the Water', who take injured service personnel competitive yacht racing. I am their Shore Manager because they helped me so much and I believe in their cause very strongly.

One person who really stands out is an unassuming guy from Weymouth called Steve

White, who originally started sailing with his best mate in a wreck of a boat without any training at all. Fast forward nine years, and Steve has completed his first Vendée Globe, known as one of the hardest sailing races in the world, finishing in eighth place! Steve re-branded his boat Toe in the Water, sailing it under that name and becoming the champion of a lot of injured service people. I was privileged to spend time with him and his family before he set off and was also there to welcome him back after he had crossed the finish line. We were greeted by a crowd of more than fifty thousand people as we sailed into port! Steve continues to help injured service personnel discover the joys of competitive sailing and looks forward to his next big adventure – the Vendée Globe 2012.

My own recovery process continues. I consider myself to be a very lucky person as there are so many people much worse off than me. Those at Headley Court humble me but also inspire me and I will do all I can to support them in the future. I thank them all, as well as everyone who has helped me personally. ∎

'I was truly honoured to be given the opportunity to sail under the banner of Toe in the Water and do my small part in promoting a worthwhile organisation. People who have heard my story have been very polite and used words like 'inspirational', but I can tell them, hand on heart, that if they want inspirational stories, stories of real courage and bravery, then they should look to people like Andy and the other injured guys and not to me.'

Steve White

Musa Qala med room 20 mins after GSW

On 19 July 2007, I was in Helmand Province, Afghanistan. We were clearing a helicopter landing site and went up to high ground to get a clear view of the area. As we reversed our vehicle to park, all of a sudden it exploded. I remember lying there with my legs shattered, and people around me screaming. I looked up to the sky and said a prayer: 'Lord Jesus, if you need to use me to motivate others about Your Kingdom, please give me back my life again.'

Back at Camp Bastion I was pronounced dead at one point but luckily one of the doctors saw a slight pulse movement. I was operated on and then taken back to the UK.

I don't remember anything about the next two weeks. Eventually I woke up and saw my wife and a doctor beside me. I asked to go to the toilet but my wife said 'I'm afraid you can't, as you have lost your legs'. I replied that I couldn't have, as I could feel that I still had my boots on and my feet were very warm.

Then I took in what she had said and asked her to come close. I said: 'If this has happened to me, let's give God the glory for my survival and help others in the same situation. Perhaps this is a new chapter in our lives.'

Now, two years later, I am taking part in athletics and sitting volleyball with Battle Back, a services organisation that helps the seriously injured. Life is for living – let's enjoy it!

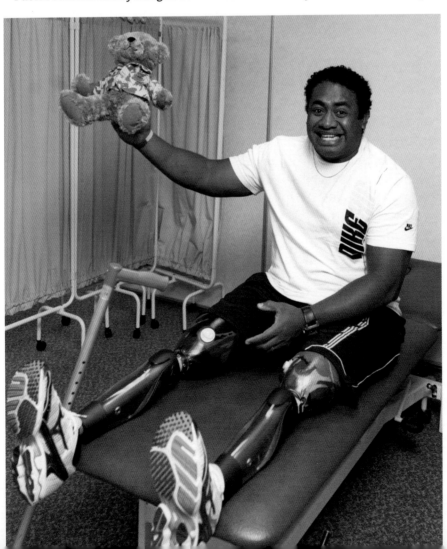

On 11 August 2007 at about 04:30 hours in Basra City, on the way back from an operation, the enemy forces contacted the patrol with an explosive formed projectile (EFP) roadside bomb and small arms fire (AK47s).

The EFP ripped through the left side of the Bulldog Armoured Fighting Vehicle and through my left shoulder. It just missed my head and the shrapnel ripped into my lower back. It paralysed my legs, and my left shoulder was taken out. Bullets were hitting the front of the vehicle and my adrenalin was pumping now and, while still under fire, I returned fire with my pistol. I then tried putting out the fire in the engine.

My hearing started to come back and I could hear my Commander, Sgt Scotty Martin, shouting and asking if I was OK. Had I been hit? I shouted back 'Yeah'. He then helped drag me into the back where the Company Medic, Steve Thorogood, stripped me down and dealt with my wounds. He offered me morphine but I said no – I wanted to know everything that was happening around me. Then the Company Sgt Major, Rob Porter, started having a giggle with me. Some funny things were said. I could hear noises. It was the blokes hooking up the blown-up Bulldog. I then got dragged back in to the Palace and then, on a stretcher, into the Med. Centre, where there were bright lights. I was met by my CO and RSM and an attractive Medical Officer. I could feel the pain and next thing I knew, I felt something hit me. I'd been given morphine so I was high as a kite. The chopper was inbound so they took me to the heli landing site and I was flown to the COB. There, I was rushed to the operating theatre where they stopped the bleeding and bandaged me up. I can't really remember much. I was still on drugs for the pain. I remember getting a brown envelope with messages all over it from Ninja 9 Platoon which cheered me up and there was a lads' mag inside it.

The Tri-Service Medic Staff were great trying to boost our morale and were dedicated to their jobs. I remember getting woken up at 0300 hours by mortars, staff were running up and down laying body armour on top of us and lowering the beds, putting themselves in danger and before even thinking about themselves. I then got flown out of Iraq to the UK, where I was driven in an ambulance to Selly Oak Hospital.

After two days, they decided what they wanted to do and took me into the operating room. I had my left shoulder replaced with metal and the shrapnel was taken out of my back. After that my Mum and Uncle came to visit every weekend and my mates and their families came too. The Red Cross looked after them all, getting them accommodation and food and travel. I had no clothes when I got there and they got me everything, even toiletries, and sorted the lads out with PSPs and other stuff. They are the unspoken heroes and I'd like to thank all of them.

It was rather depressing being in hospital for a long time but you all stick together. That's what we do best and help your mucker out. We used to go down to the front of A&E on Friday nights with a hot chocolate and watch all the funny drunk people come in. I then went to Headley Court and had physio. After that I returned to my unit where all my mates were and had some well-earned banter with them.

It took me almost a year to regain my fitness but I had a strong mind and willpower. I've lost some movement and strength which I won't get back and I've got a metal shoulder now, but I won't let that stop me.

I'm still with 4 Rifles and proud to be an infantry front line soldier. I'm due to redeploy to the front line in Afghan in the near future. ◼

Russ Laye & Jim Davidson

In March 2002, I was serving as a Petty Officer Medical Assistant in Royal Navy Sick Quarters, HMS Drake. I was preparing to leave the Navy and continue as a rig medic, working for more money for fewer hours. I was also a keen motorcyclist and the treasurer for the Plymouth branch of the Royal Navy Motorcycle Club.

On the evening of the accident, my colleague, Matt, and I were on our way to a pub called the Plume of Feathers in Princetown to put down a deposit for a weekend social event that I was organising. However, it was a journey that I never completed. An elderly chap decided to pull out of a side road and BANG... I went over the bonnet and Matt ended up dead on the side of the road. This is when all the plans went out the window. And the greatest challenge I have ever faced began.

I woke up a week later in the High Dependency Unit in Derriford Hospital with a smashed pelvis and right leg.

Fast forward to several months later and I'm referred to a wonderful place called Headley Court. This is the tri-Service Rehabilitation Unit in the South of England, where I got, not only the physical help I needed, but the mental help, which is so important following any major traumatic incident. The biggest motivation I had at the time was the fact that Matt had died. I was broken, but I was alive. I just had to get myself stronger and walking again, unaided. I'm still working on that one.

I'm currently semi-retired and able to walk only with the aid of a stick – sometimes, on a bad day, with two sticks. And I choose to spend all my available time working for the charity **Help for Heroes**. It's my way of paying back everything they gave me. Whilst I was in Headley, I saw a poster which read:

'Minds are like parachutes; they only work when they are open'

That is now the way I look at life. I have also discovered the most important thing in life, and I'm not going to tell you what it is, as every one will find it one day. I visit the local gym at least four times a week and am in training so that I can take part in the 2010 sponsored cycle ride.

There are several people who, over the years have always inspired me, and my favourite would be **Mr Jim Davidson**. I first saw him live on stage whilst I was on board HMS Falmouth in the Falklands. We were so keen to see his show that we rammed the fleet auxiliary that he was doing the show on! So why, in this day and age, does Jim Davidson get my vote? The world has become a very dangerous place for those in the media spotlight, and many bend to those pressures not wanting to offend certain people. But there are a few strong-willed individuals who are not afraid to be honest and say exactly what they mean. And Jim is one of them. There is no need for me to go on about the fantastic work that he has done in the past for the Forces including the BFF.

Final thought: Don't worry – be happy! ▪

I joined the REME as a Mechanic in 1997. I had ten years of active service and two further years of recovering, which involved twelve operations and 100 hours of surgery.

I was in Iraq on 6 December 2006. We went out on patrol with B Company Green Jackets – now The Rifles. We had a contact. As we went to pull out of the area, a vehicle broke down and we went to collect it. The enemy suspected it was a broken-down vehicle and put some fire down on it. My crew and I attached it to my vehicle with the recovery equipment. As we went to pull out of the area, I had to pop my head up to see through the dust for the driver. At that point, a sniper shot me through the face. I dropped down into my one-man turret and realised I was in a bad way. I bandaged up my face and held my airway open by putting my thumb in my mouth and pushing my palate up a bit. Then it was wacky races back to the hospital! The Company Sergeant Major jumped on top of the vehicle and commanded it back to the hospital at Basra Palace. At the hospital, I climbed out of the vehicle on my own and then the medics put me on the stretcher. I woke up three weeks later at Selly Oaks, Birmingham, with my family at my side.

I spoke to my Grandma on the phone. She was dying of lung cancer, and she inspired me, as she was more worried about me than about herself.

After Christmas, I was given news of a few friends who had died in combat and, at that point, I decided I could not sulk about being injured – at least I had come home. The training and the life I had led before gave me the strength of heart and willpower to get on with it and survive. I am eternally grateful for the support I received from so many people throughout my ordeal.

I have always idolised **Barrie McDermott** because of his rugby career and what people have said about his character. To realise he achieved it all with just one eye, made him more remarkable to me. And then, when I lost my sight (I have only ten per cent in one eye), I got great support from him and things to cheer me up – tickets, signed shirt etc. I realised that, if he could achieve what he had, then there was a chance I could live a normal life too.

Barrie works for communities now, for disadvantaged kids – and that is what I am starting to do. I am most of the way through a teaching qualification and I would like to work with young people, using my experiences to help them achieve their potential.

I enjoyed my time in the Forces and was very sorry to leave.

'I received a letter from one of my squaddy mates a few years ago, telling me of Simon's injuries. He thought that, because I'd lost the sight in my right eye as a kid, we would have lots in common. When I found out how Simon's injuries had happened, I was shocked, but I decided to show my support because Simon was an unrelenting Leeds fan.

It wasn't long before I met Simon and, once I had, I realised how positive he was. I was inspired by his outlook on life – and, for Simon to say kind words about me, I consider a great privilege and honour.

Before my accident at the age of fifteen, I had planned to join the Army (Paras). I had always been a bit of a scrapper and a fighter and I figured that, if I had a weapon in my hand, I'd have a bloody good chance of winning the argument!

Simon is the type of bloke I would have spent all my time with, at work, rest and play, because he's a top bloke with a great sense of duty and integrity. He's got a shit sense of humour, but hopefully he won't be making his living as a stand-up comedian!

So for now, mate, carry on being yourself... a hero.

Barrie McDermott
Leeds Rhinos

Barrie McDermott, born 22 July 1972, is a former English Rugby League footballer. His position was prop-forward. Barrie is now the Head of Youth Development with his former club, Leeds Rhinos, and appears as a pundit on Sky Sports.

Admiral Sir Jonathon Band GCB ADC First Sea Lord and Chief of Naval Staff

In making the world a safer place, members of our Armed Forces can and have paid a high personal price, not only emotionally, but also physically and mentally – we owe a huge debt of gratitude to each and every one, and their families. Capturing the public mood, **Help for Heroes** was formed specifically with this in mind and, since its inception continues, in conjunction with other established service charities, to support wounded service personnel and their families as they come to terms with life-changing injuries and personal trauma. Their achievements are remarkable and, in consequence, **Help for Heroes** continues to make a positive and tangible difference at a time when it is most needed. The Royal Navy is profoundly grateful for the level of practical support and national pride which **Help for Heroes** has helped to engender for our Armed Forces. Whilst the pages of this book recount personal tales of sacrifice, adversity and personal achievement, as a whole it provides a fitting tribute to all of our servicemen and women, capturing the comradeship and spirit of thousands of heroes who are currently serving around the world. Whilst it is a humbling insight into the lives of some who have paid a personal price to keep us safe, you will also be inspired and uplifted by the determination and resilience of the human spirit, whose instinct is to survive, adapt, and to strive to overcome what can appear at times to be the impossible. ■

I was in 1st Battalion Welsh Guards and served in Northern Ireland, the Falklands, Berlin, Kenya and on public duties based in England between 1977–1984.

On 8 June 1982, whilst serving in the Falklands, we got attacked by Sky Hawk jets and they hit the ship with a 500lb bomb, killing 48 and injuring 97 – me included.

I received 48 per cent burns and was taken to Queen Elizabeth Military Hospital in Woolwich where I spent five years, on and off.

Help for Heroes is a wonderful charity and I just wish somebody had thought about it when we were injured. It would have been great! ▇

Please Give Generously

I never realised that after eight years in the Army, my career would be brought to an end like it was.

I joined the Parachute Regiment when I was 18 and experienced some brilliant and dangerous times. Whilst fighting in Afghanistan, I sustained five gunshot wounds.

Whilst moving forward clearing enemy positions, I was shot in the thigh. The pure force of that three-inch bullet forced me back, spun me round and threw me on the ground. As daft as it sounds, I did not realise what had happened. Eventually, I looked down to see that my leg had swollen to twice its normal size. Bullets were landing all around me. As I tried to drag my injured leg behind cover I got hit for the second time.

As two mates came to my aid, I got hit through my chest webbing twice, which set it on fire. I was dragged back to safety and I can remember looking at the enemy and thinking 'one more to the head or chest and that's me over'. Luckily, they only hit me in the hip.

As my eyes started to get heavy, I can remember feeling the down-draught of the helicopter. I looked up to see the blurry rotary blades and I felt safe. I closed my eyes and woke up four days later in Selly Oak Hospital.

On waking up, I was hallucinating about friends and colleagues. I had forgotten about the injuries until the consultant spoke to me. He said, 'Stu, you're safe. You're going to be OK, but the damage to your ankle means it is too severe to save. I think the best option is to look at removing the leg below the knee. I'll come back in ten minutes. Have a chat with Lisa and let me know your decision'. I went into total shock and was physically sick. Lisa was my girlfriend. She and I had had little life experience, but now we had to make that massive decision.

I have undergone many years of physical and mental rehabilitation since then. Circumstances like mine did not only affect me, but a huge number of family and friends around me. Through it all I just feel lucky to be alive. I am now married to Lisa, we have two wonderful children, but there was a point when this very nearly did not happen.

I think we all face challenges in life, but it's how we deal with, and come to terms with, these challenges that defines who we really are.

'I think we all face challenges in life, but it's how we deal with, and come to terms with, these challenges that defines who we really are.'

Steve Rowley Magic Act & Children's Entertainer

Whirlwind Entertainments grew from Steve Rowley's lifelong passion for drama and entertainment. Having been involved in party entertainment and performance from a very early age, starting a party entertainment and decoration business was the realisation of a personal ambition.

As a small child, Steve became interested in performing magic tricks, and quickly became well-known in the children's entertainment business. By the age of thirteen, Steve had created Steve's Party Magic, which offered hour-long shows. Five years later, Steve established his company, and formed Whirlwind Entertainments.

Steve says, 'Putting a smile on someone's face is priceless and the satisfaction you receive in return is incredible. Being an entertainer, I receive this amazing fulfilment on a daily basis and such a little thing can bring so much happiness to an individual.

'This is why my support for the **Help for Heroes** campaign is so strong. Not only are they dedicated to creating the best facilities and magnificent rehabilitation centres. They put a smile on the faces of amazing people who have risked everything for one reason... their country.'

Michael Egan, Gary Tide, Kevin Tyson, Lee Carol, Daniel Graham, Jamie Casey, Danny Powers, Timmy Dane, Ryan Canning, Eddy Williams, Dan Fritzal, Jason Cane, Raymond Smith, Jimmy Reps and others...

We are a group of English-born lads, who are extremely proud of our country and St George.

This year was no different as the lads from all over London, and myself, took to Trafalgar Square to celebrate our National Day.

I think it's crazy that, despite the fact that St George has been the patron saint of England since the 14th century, most people don't even know that St George's Day falls on 23 April.

We are extremely proud of our patriotism and our saint. We are working men of England with a passion to celebrate the history that lies behind our country.

We are all backing our boys and the **Help for Heroes** charity. ▨

I joined the Army in August 2001 and, on completion of training, I joined the 2nd Battalion The Royal Green Jackets. I served in Northern Ireland in 2005. Then, in 2007, the Royal Green Jackets amalgamated to form the Rifles. I was then part of 4th Battalion The Rifles and, in April of the same year, I was deployed to Basra Palace, Iraq, on Op Telic 10.

During the Battalion's time in the Palace, we experienced some of the worst fighting the British Army had seen in decades.

While we were in Basra, a charity called **Help For Heroes** was started.

Upon our return from Iraq, a friend and I

wanted to do something for this charity to help it support our friends and comrades who had been injured, whether at home or on Operations.

We started last summer by collecting donations and selling the **Help for Heroes** wristbands in large shopping centres. After this, we decided that we wanted to do something that we would remember, as well as helping our friends at the same time. One night, over a beer, we were talking about doing a coast-to-coast walk. This then spiralled into walking a mile for each service person who lost their life as a result of serving in Afghanistan and Iraq. We also decided that our finishing point should be one of the best known places of remembrance in the United Kingdom – The Cenotaph.

We spoke to **Help for Heroes** and decided to walk around the garrisons that have connections to the Service or to the Regiments that have suffered the most from these conflicts. So the most prominent places we wanted to visit were Colchester, Brize Norton, Larkhill, Tidworth, Exeter, Poole, Portsmouth, Winchester, Aldershot and London.

We know that the money we raised will help the continued efforts of this charity that supports our injured heroes and their families. ▮

The Royal Marines **End-to-End Challenge**

Why did we do it?

Whilst serving at the Headquarters of Multinational Division SouthEast (Iraq), we were seeing our fellow Marines and servicemen paying a rather more hefty price for serving in Afghanistan.

In order to support them, Major Mike Scanlon came up with the idea of a large charity event in order to help those who needed it upon their return. Being Royal Marines, it would have to be a physical challenge.

There are few greater challenges on mainland Great Britain than making one's way along the full length of the country and so the John O'Groats to Land's End (JOGLE) concept was born.

Even this was not enough of a challenge, however, and two further events were hit upon – abseiling down both the Blackpool Tower and the Avon Gorge in Bristol (this time with our bicycles attached!). The entire journey took us along a route of 901 miles and it was completed in 58 hours, over ten days. ∎

My name is Joe Townsend. I was injured while serving with 40 Commando Royal Marines while on tour in Afghanistan in 2008.

It was the 8 February 2008 when we patrolled out of FOB Gib. From what I can remember, we had left on an early morning patrol to push into the Green Zone, hoping to catch the Taliban IED teams who had been laying devices in the area. It was a long exhausting patrol, but so was every patrol we had been on. We were patrolling back to the FOB after numerous hours on the ground. My section was point section for the Company and I was point man in the section. Only 800m from the FOB we broke through a tree line and I began to patrol through the ploughed fields between us and Gib. I picked a random route, as we always did when patrolling, and next thing I knew I was in the air and there was a cloud of grey smoke surrounding me.

My ears were ringing and I was confused as to what was going on. I had landed on my back and realised I had been blown up. I managed to prop myself up into a sitting position against my day sack. I looked down to see one of my boots missing and the other one pretty mangled. I could feel a funny sensation in my legs but felt no pain. I turned to the man to my rear and said

'Oh, cheers Pusser', a quote that had been used comically many a time in Delta Coy. I reached across with my left arm to try and get into my medical pouch to get my tourniquets, but, as hard as I tried to pull on the strap fastening the pouch, it wouldn't open. Looking back now I realise it was because my left arm had also been shattered in the blast. Luckily the section medic was attached to the rear of my section and he got to me instantly. He proceeded to patch me up and tourniquet both my legs and my arm. I was later told he had used over 20 first field dressings to prevent me from bleeding to death. The lads got

> **The whole family are immensely proud of Joe and what he has achieved so far. At long last, Joe's dream has come true and we are looking forward to starting to build his new bungalow where he will be able to live an independent life.**
>
> David Carter, Joe Townsend's grandfather

me onto a stretcher whilst we waited for the helicopter to CASEVAC me. I remember everything from the blast until I got on the helicopter, when I assume I was drugged up.

My troop medic saved my life that day.

The only other snippet I remember was when I got back to Bastion. I saw the Padre and he asked me how I was. I replied 'I seem to be having problems locating my legs, Sir'.

The next thing I remember, I was in ITU in Selly Oak Hospital, back in the UK. After being under for a week, I came round to see my Dad and my brother at the end of my bed. My first words were

'What the f... are you doing out here?' The nurse asked me if I knew who these people were. I replied 'Yes. That's my Dad and my little brother.' I thought that I was still in Afghanistan.

I can't remember my reaction when I was told, but I had lost both my legs and there was a struggle to keep my arm. I spent just under five months in Selly Oak Hospital, which was the hardest thing I have ever done.

I moved down to Headley Court from Selly Oak, which was a massive lift for me, and, within ten days of being there, I was stood upright on my first set of stubbies (prosthetic training legs).

I have come on so much since being at Headley Court. I have been walking, although still struggling, driving a car and living independently. I am still a patient at Headley and still returning to Selly Oak for surgery but all of this is for a positive outcome. With a few more operations, I hope to be clear of further surgery and be up on my prostheses comfortably.

For me, losing my legs hasn't changed the person I am or what I can do. I wouldn't say there is anything that I can't do now which I could before. All it takes is thinking of a way round things and using grit and determination to do it. It might take me a lot longer and a lot more effort but I will do it.

Recently I have been fighting with the local council for planning permission to build a specially adapted bungalow to suit my needs. The support throughout the nation to get the proposed planning refusal turned around just shows the support for our British Forces.

Also, my family have had a big part to play in the fight for my planning but, more importantly, my road to rehabilitation. Without the support of my family, friends and colleagues I wouldn't be where I am now. Thank you all. ▮

Why did I choose **Help for Heroes**?

I am a student at Derby University in Buxton. I am studying a Foundation Degree (Arts) in Public Services. Alongside this, I am also enrolled on the Derby Award scheme, which is a management and leadership course. As part of the award scheme, I was asked to put on an event for a charity of my choice, in order to demonstrate my management and leadership skills.

I am a member of the local Volunteer Lifesaving Club, whose main aims are to teach people how to save lives in the water, whether it be at home or out on the sea, and how to keep themselves safe near and around water. What we decided to do was a Sponsored Swimathon. We arranged it at the Sovereign Centre, Eastbourne. We swam as many lengths as we could. We all enjoyed it and we raised funds for our chosen charity, **Help for Heroes**.

I chose to raise money for **Help for Heroes** because I wanted to help make a difference to the lives of our injured servicemen and women.

A few of my friends are in the Armed Forces and I know of others too. I would hate to think that, should any of them be injured or disabled through serving our country, that we, general members of the public, could not do something to help compensate them.

Joe Townsend was one of my main reasons for choosing **Help for Heroes**.

I attended the same school as Joe, and I studied Public Services at the same college as he did. When I heard what had happened to him, I thought 'Why him? Why?' But I couldn't answer that. I just didn't know.

Joe went out on tour with the Marines, not knowing when, or if, he would come back – let alone knowing that he would suffer such awful injuries. But, as with all heroes, he has bravely borne his injuries and is an inspiration to us all. ■

Beefeaters

Hayley Mac Miss UK Galaxy 2009

Help for Heroes is all about people 'doing their bit'! We are ex-servicemen and women doing our bit having served our country with courage and distinction. We continue to show our support for those that currently serve. ■

My good friend was killed in Afghanistan recently but I don't think anyone needs a reason to get involved with **Help for Heroes**, it's such a great charity and we should all look after our troops. ■

The Royal Air Force deeply appreciates the superb support **Help For Heroes** has provided to personnel injured in the line of duty. There is a long tradition in the United Kingdom of public generosity and charitable support to the services, including through the established service charities, but the achievements of **Help for Heroes** have been remarkable, both in terms of the amount and speed with which money has been raised. **Help for Heroes** has captured the imagination of the general public but I would also pay tribute to the injured servicemen and women, some of whose stories are contained in this book, who have worked tirelessly to raise awareness and funding for injured colleagues.

As well as support for injured personnel, I believe **Help for Heroes** has also had a hugely positive impact on the public's understanding of the challenges our servicemen and women face on current operations. As memories of previous conflicts and National Service diminish, there are fewer and fewer people who understand the realities of military life, and the sacrifices our people are asked to make on behalf of the country. Support for **Help for Heroes** has gone a long way to rectifying that situation.

On behalf of the Royal Air Force, I would like to thank everyone who has contributed to **Help for Heroes** and to those who were the inspiration behind the organisation, for their generosity, commitment and interest in the welfare of our servicemen and women. It has been a truly remarkable effort and an outstanding success. ■

> **'Help for Heroes has captured the imagination of the general public...'**

Pam Garland **Husky sledding in Norway**

In January 2009, my son was very seriously injured in Afghanistan whilst serving with the British Army. He had only been in the country for ten weeks and it was his first tour.

We were devastated to get the 'knock on the door' that all parents and loved ones of servicemen and women, serving in a war zone, dread.

Whilst at Selly Oak Hospital we were all extremely well looked after by various charities that have all received donations from **Help for Heroes**. We saw a large number of very badly injured Servicemen at Selly Oak, and for the above reasons I wanted to raise as much money as possible for **Help for Heroes** to assist and support our wounded service personnel.

Fortunately my son is making a good recovery... some are not so lucky.

To raise funds for **Help for Heroes** to support all those brave men and women who were injured in Iraq and Afghanistan, I decided to go dog sledding for five days in the wilds of northern Norway, leaving from Alta.

This, the ultimate challenge for me, required a good level of fitness and stamina with long eight-hour days in temperatures of down to minus 30 degrees, crossing over 220kms of frozen wasteland with my own team of four Siberian huskies. This might sound like a nice journey in the snow with the dogs doing all the work but this was not the case. I was running alongside the dogs, pushing and pulling the sled up and down hills to help them.

The odyssey of ice and teamwork between human and dog provided a huge challenge for me mentally and physically but, more importantly, it allowed me to support and highlight a great cause, which means so very much to me. ▪

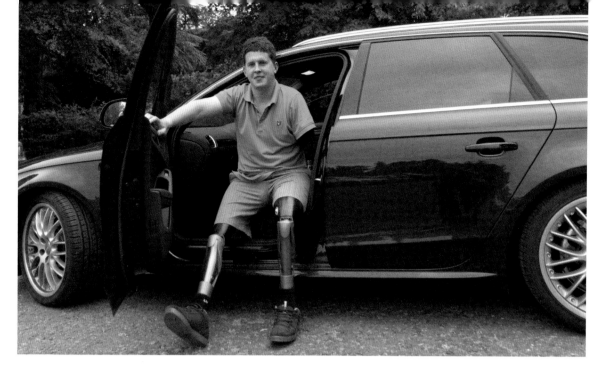

Corporal Thomas Neathway 2nd Battalion The Parachute Regiment, Patrols Platoon

I joined the Army in December 2001. I have served in Northern Ireland, and twice in Iraq and Afghanistan. I was a sniper in Patrols Platoon in Afghanistan. I got injured on 22 July 2008 in Kajaki. I was on a routine patrol where we would patrol out and observe the Taliban until we got a reaction. Then we would smash them. On this day, however, on moving into the compound which had been cleared with metal detectors, I went to move down into a position which was a hole in the wall in the corner of the compound. This was a good place to observe from and see through. In front of this hole was a sandbag. I moved the sandbag, which detonated a booby trap device. It instantly took my legs off and my left arm was badly damaged. Lance Corporal Jan Fourie, the medic, came over, carried out immediate first aid and began to Casevac (Casualty Evacuation) me out to HLS (Helicopter Landing Site). I knew how badly I was hurt but I knew I'd be OK because my mates would get me out. I lost consciousness as the helicopter arrived and woke up a few days later in the Intensive Care Unit at Selly Oak Hospital, Birmingham. The first thing I noticed when I woke up was that my left arm had been amputated, which I was gutted about for about ten minutes. And then I realised I just needed to get on with things. I had plenty of friends and family around me then, and through my whole stay at Selly Oak. I started thinking about the Afghanistan Tour of Duty Presentation which was going to be held at my Regiment's base in Colchester, and I decided to work towards getting out of my wheelchair and walking to receive my medal. It wasn't hard to do in my mind but it was hard to be able to do it physically. It took me two months of great effort and probably should have taken much longer. I have the same life now as I had before – only now I am in a wheelchair. I still go out at the weekend on the lash with my mates. Now I just want to crack on. My next goal will be to get back to work. That's it! ▮

The Rt Revd Bob Evens, Bishop of Crediton
Here in Devon, we are proud of the men and women in our Armed Forces who serve our country overseas. This Vintage Tractor Run shows how ordinary people can offer practical support for those who have been bereaved or wounded and who need our continuing care. If the Government is unwilling to meet their needs, then it is up to us to do all we can, so that their courage and sacrifice is not forgotten.

'**Most people don't appreciate what our Armed Forces do for us. It is such a good cause that we felt we should donate the proceeds of this year's Tractor Run to** Help for Heroes.'
Arthur Parsons

Tigger Howarth
I did 22 years in the Royal Corps of Signals as a Radio Supervisor. I served in Bosnia, Germany, Cyprus, Northern Ireland, the Falkland Islands and Belize. I am a country boy, born and bred in Dalwood, East Devon. I believe in keeping country traditions alive and, although not a farmer's son, I own five tractors as well as some classic motor-bikes. I feel that not enough is done for our troops by our elected Government so the **Help for Heroes** charity is a fantastic worthwhile cause in which many different and varied groups of people can show their support for our 'heroes'. ■

Flossy Quinn

I wanted to do this jump to raise awareness for **Help for Heroes** and for all the brave people who still soldier on, even though their lives have been shattered.

Soldiers give their lives to protect people, and it makes me angry when I hear stories on the news of people not supporting and encouraging them.

Wars didn't mean anything to me until my brother joined the Army. But when he left home for the first time, it scared me and suddenly I realised that every soldier had a family who worried about what the future held for them. I had seen interviews with soldiers on television who had lost limbs and been traumatised by what they had experienced. **Help for Heroes** helps to rebuild these men's lives.

I felt really scared before the jump. It's a daunting feeling jumping from 14,000 feet, but it is nothing in comparison to what soldiers do every day.

It was a truly amazing experience. Cool!

Michael Dauncey

I am 89 years old and won two tickets at a **Help for Heroes** raffle at Old Sarum Airfield in 2008 to parachute with the Red Devils. So I thought, why not?! I took my son, John, with me, and it was a brilliant, fantastic experience. I felt so lucky to meet such kind and thoughtful men as the Red Devils.

Melissa Rolfe

I decided to jump with the Red Devils for my brother, Private Peter Cowton, who sadly lost his life in July 2008 whilst serving with 2 Paras in Afghanistan. It was fun and very exhilarating, and I felt that Pete was there with me. ▮

Top: LCpl Phil Webley, LCpl Danny Kelly, Sgt Jay Webster, Flossy Quinn, LCpl Nathe Connolly, LCpl Jimmy Graham.
Centre: Sgt Jay Webster, Melissa Rolfe.
Below: Michael Dauncey, LCpl Nathe Connolly, John Dauncey.

How do you raise money for **Help for Heroes**? It's a simple recipe really.

First of all you will need four schoolchildren, four soldiers and two firefighters.

Add free jam doughnuts and coke/coffee/tea, to taste, to warm the volunteers.

Prepare a fire engine with full water tanks, and attach fire hoses as necessary.

Prepare several buckets of soapy water and sponges.

Add the children, soldiers and firefighters into the mix and stand well back.

If it all gets too childish, remove soldiers and allow to simmer for a while before returning to the mix once more!

LCpl Ben Wedlake, Spr Billy Parker, Spr Richard Parton and Spr Arwel Jones from 42 Engineer Regiment (Geographic) based in Newbury would like to say a massive 'thank you' to Newbury Fire Station and the children of St Bartholomew's School for allowing us to join in your fund-raising activities for **Help for Heroes**.

Many of our Regiment have served in both Iraq and Afghanistan and know what an overwhelming difference the money raised by **Help for Heroes** makes to our wounded.

We are proud to have been able to assist the local community in fund-raising and would like to say thank you for all the money collected.

Luke Wilson, Ross Collington, Lewis Rogers and Macaulay Gill (four of the 'ingredients' in the above mix) had the following comments to make about their endeavour:

'I think it's really important to support the soldiers who have been wounded protecting our country.'

'Our soldiers defend our country's reputation and it's about time we did something in return.'

'I think it's important because we wouldn't be here without them.'

'We chose this charity because the soldiers that get wounded deserve something, as it can ruin their lives.'

I am currently serving as a Weapons Technician in the Royal Air Force and hold the rank of Senior Aircraftsman Technician 'SAC(T)'. I am based at RAF Cottesmore and this was my parent station when I deployed to Basra in May 2007. I joined 903EAW which was the RAF formed unit. My role was to support Operations, especially the Joint Force Helicopter. It was when I was on my way to work at Basra Airport that the siren sounded and the base came under Indirect Fire (IDF) attack. I was hit by a 240mm rocket which lacerated my left arm. I was evacuated to Basra Field Hospital where they saved my life, but, consequently, I lost my arm. The amputation was above-elbow.

I was flown back to the UK where I stayed at Selly Oak Hospital and then transferred to Headley Court, where I continued my rehabilitation. There, I learnt how to use a prosthetic arm and had physiotherapy on my shoulder to give me the ability to use the arm to its full capabilities. All in all, my rehab lasted only four months before I was discharged and went on sick leave pending my Return Back-to-Work programme. When I went back to work I was put behind a desk – something I wasn't used to. This was very frustrating: no challenges, not enough work to go round and I missed engineering. I started questioning my future within the Armed Forces.

It was about six months ago when I decided that enough was enough. I wasn't happy in my job and I couldn't see it changing any time soon, let alone as far as a full career. My Medical Board approached and by this point I had already made my mind up. I was going to leave the services. I got a medical discharge 18 February 2009 and I am due to leave the service later this year.

Whilst I was at work, I had the opportunity to think what I was going to do when I left.

I didn't know what job I wanted and Further Education appealed to me. I applied through UCAS for university and I have since been accepted for Law at Manchester Metropolitan.

Since receiving my injury I haven't really looked back. I've had my highs and lows but most of them have been highs. It has been a life-changing experience and, hopefully, one for the better. I have been reasonably fit all my life. I couldn't continue with my love for Thai boxing or some aspects of gym work, so I was on the lookout for new sports. I went to a Paralympics 'taster day' at Loughborough University in November 2007, where I tried out a whole range of sports. Cycling was the last one I tried and the coaches said I had potential. I didn't follow it up for many reasons but I watched the Olympics and focussed on the cycling. Chris Hoy stood out from the rest of the competitors and made it exciting for viewers to watch. It spurred me on to try for the Paralympics again. After getting back in touch with the coaches, I went to Newport to a development camp to ride the track. I enjoyed the weekend but then had to wait to see if I could take my ambition further. A couple of weeks later, while I was skiing with 'Battle Back', I got a phone call asking if I would like to join the Paralympics Development Programme. I am now training full-time to try to get into the Paralympics squad and, who knows, maybe London 2012.

My family have always been there to support me through the bad as well as the good and I wouldn't be where I am now without them.

Meeting Chris Hoy was amazing. He was down to earth and really easy to talk to. ∎

'It was great to meet Jon-Allan at the Manchester Velodrome and I was really pleased to hear that the success of the British cyclists during the Beijing Olympics and Paralympics last year has inspired him to take up the sport.

When we met, back in April, he'd just found out that he'd been accepted onto the Para-Cycling Development Programme, which is fantastic news, and I wish him the very best of luck.'

Sir Chris Hoy

Radford Family Centre Ladies' Charity Event

After a chat at our weekly coffee morning at the Radford Family Centre, a small group of wives, girlfriends, mums and friends of service personnel, and one lone husband whose wife was away in Afghanistan, decided that it would be a great idea to raise some money for **Help for Heroes**, an amazing charity which is close to all our hearts.

We are reminded almost every day in the media what devastation is caused to the lives of injured members of our Armed Forces and, as we were talking, it became apparent that we all knew of someone or had heard of someone who had been injured whilst serving their country – whether on the front line in Afghanistan or deep under the sea in a submarine.

The idea was hit upon that, as our guys had completed an assault course as part of their training before leaving, then that is what we would do. Little did we realise just how much more we would end up doing!

After an early panic at the beginning of the week when the coach company pulled out, leaving everyone to wonder how they were all going to get there, a quick appeal on the local radio network answered all our prayers when Target Travel stepped in and gave us a coach and driver for free.

On a bright and sunny Saturday morning, early in May 2009, 40 wives, girlfriends and daughters, with ages ranging from 16 to 50, met at the Radford, and marched down the road to meet the

> The Help for Heroes charity gives valuable and much needed support to our Armed Services.
>
> As most of our staff have close links with the services, either through family or because we are ex-service personnel ourselves, it was a great opportunity to help the ladies from the Radford Family Centre in their fundraising.
>
> Being able to offer the venue and activities for their event, we hope that the charity and, subsequently, the Armed Forces personnel themselves, will benefit in some small way.

Mountain Water Experience Limited:
Director Mark Agnew, Chief Instructor Jenny Lord

coach, to begin a day of activities at the Mountain Water Experience in Kingsbridge, Devon.

A full day of activities ensued – climbing a Jacob's Ladder, a Climbing Wall, Crate Stacking, Traversing on a Zip Wire, Archery and an Assault Course. We were split into four teams and the rivalry was rife! It was an amazing day, but in the back of all our minds was the reason why we were there.

All those who attended thoroughly enjoyed themselves and at the evening function at the Family Centre the main topic of conversation was 'who had the best bruises'. Evening entertainment was supplied, again free of charge, by 'Blues Highway' and DJ Andy D. A raffle and charity auction boosted the funds. ▪

When I deployed to Afghanistan, I was serving with 40 Commando Royal Marines. I had a great time with C Company in charge of a fire team in a close combat section. We were sent to protect the hydro-electric dam at Kajaki, Helmand Province. After getting settled in to the patrol routine, I managed to get myself shot, six weeks into the tour.

The Company was on a standard morning patrol. After a long slog, we reached the furthest point to which we were to go, not coming under contact. As the troop ahead of us were a bound forward, the sections of my troop put up protection from the cover of rooftops to allow the point troop to come back through ours. On the roof with me were two guys from my fire team – my GPMG Gunner and my UGL Gunner.

After a couple of minutes we received light inaccurate fire. Desperate to 'ping' the firing points we stayed to see if we could locate the enemy. Then, all of a sudden, my GPMG gunner, Ben, threw me off the roof. As the dust settled, Ben called over and said he thought he had broken his ankle. I tried to stand up to help him but searing pain in my right foot made me realise that I had been shot through the ankle. This was given away by two little red dots either side of my desert boot.

At this point, Ben realised he had been shot too! The rest of the team came to our aid and checked on Nick, the third bloke, who was still under fire and had been shot through both legs!

During our extraction, another Marine was shot through his arse and out through his thigh. The lads now had four casualties to deal with in the middle of a heavy fire fight.

Hats off to the lads! They carried us on stretchers till they were sick from physical exertion, and put themselves in great danger.

I think that is what makes the Marines so special – their ability to carry out tasks to such a high standard, with a sense of disregard for their own safety.

After an hour crawling, hopping, dragging and running, we reached the pick-up point where we met the Sergeant Major, on his quad, with a trailer. Two at a time, he drove us up a wide wadi, twice, with no cover and in full view of the enemy, to get us to the helicopter extraction point.

I remember laughing on the helicopter, looking at Ben, as we breathed the gas the medics gave us. Somehow we had made it out of there – thanks entirely to the lads in the Company.

At Bastion I had the wound cleaned and, in a few hours, we were on a plane back to the UK.

At Selly Oak Hospital, the surgeons tried to rebuild my ankle and I had an external fixator bolted into my leg and foot to stabilise the joint. This was removed and I began eleven months of rehab. Unfortunately, to no avail. I was left with the choice of fusion or amputation. I opted for the latter, as I thought it would best enable me to carry on leading an active lifestyle.

I think we all choose to do the jobs we do and sometimes we pay the price. My time at Headley Court has made me realise that actually, my injury is just a scratch compared with those suffered by so many other guys – and now girls – and I'm lucky with what I have got!

I have great plans for the future. We'll see if they come about. In the meantime, I'm running over a few little obstacles that are in the way, but there's nothing that can't be cracked and hopefully I can lead a normal life just like anyone else. ▐

Jodie Cross, Lydia's mother, writes: In 2003, our two daughters contracted different strains of meningitis with septicaemia within two weeks of each other. Both Millie, then aged eight months, and Lydia, aged two and three quarters, were on life support machines, with multi-organ failure. Millie made a full recovery to the amazement of the specialists.

Lydia, unfortunately, wasn't quite so lucky. We were told that she would lose her arms, legs, cheeks, the tip of her nose and her lips. Luckily, everything recovered apart from her legs. The only option was for Lydia to have below-knee double amputations.

Despite countless ups and downs over the years, one thing that has never changed is that Lydia will never be beaten. What anyone else can do, she will have a go at. She rides a bike without stabilisers, surfs on her knees, walks along a beam at gymnastics, jumps off, landing on her feet. She climbs trees, rides her scooter and swims without her legs on.

She very rarely complains; I don't think she knows what self-pity is. She has acquired a unique sense of humour, and is able to laugh at things she does or situations she's in.

Tony, Lydia's Dad, is the Devon representative for **Help for Heroes**. Tony used to be a commando in the Army but is now a policeman. Both the girls wanted to know what the charity was all about and Lydia went on to the website to find out more.

Totally her own idea, she decided to do a sponsored swim. We told her that it would be difficult and would mean hard work. At first, she said she wanted to do nine lengths of the pool. As she was seven at the time, I thought it would be a good idea if she did seven, but Maggie, her swimming teacher, said she could do at least 20.

I couldn't believe it; I thought there was no way she could do that amount. The swim was arranged to take place on Lydia's eighth birthday, 25 February 2009. This gave her about six weeks to train up for it.

Lydia has to have the bones trimmed in her legs, usually every 12–18 months, because, as she grows, they grow in pointed spurs and push at the bottom of her legs. This prevents her from wearing her prosthesis and results in her having to spend long periods of time in her wheelchair or walking around on her knees. Happily, as the sponsored swim was to take place during one of those times when she was off her legs, waiting for surgery, it gave her something else to focus on.

Unfortunately though, the operation was scheduled to take place on her birthday, which meant postponing the swim. Two weeks later, an infection in her leg required yet another operation. So, the swim was rescheduled for 20 May 2009.

A week before this, Lydia was thrilled to meet and swim with Tom Daley. He was lovely and told her 'nothing is impossible' – which must have given Lydia the idea that no way was she going to do only 20 lengths!

Matt Kingston very kindly came to watch and support Lydia during her swim.

He was fantastic with our two girls. Having him there at the pool side, with family and friends cheering her on, inspired Lydia to swim a whole mile, 64 lengths in 64 minutes!

The reason why she was so motivated to do this was quite simply, in her own words, 'Because they have got leggies like mine, and I want to help them'. ▟

Opposite: Lydia Cross with Matt Kingston

My name is Chris Devine and I am a Combat Medical Technician in 225 Scottish Medical Regiment (V).

Our Regiment has entered six teams into the 'Heroes Challenge' which is a 29-mile walk in under 12 hours, ending at Melrose Rugby Club.

We have members of the Regiment currently on OPS in Afghanistan and our unit, 231 Medical Evacuation Squadron, has four soldiers on OPS. Our way of supporting them is to try and raise as much money as we can.

Help for Heroes is an amazing concept with its support for all serving and ex-serving soldiers. I served in the regular infantry in the 1990s and I wish we had had this kind of support. ■

Will Kemble Clarkson **The Mongol Derby**

I've always been in awe of men and women who volunteer to put themselves in harm's way so that they might protect people they may never meet, people like me. All politics aside, what our Armed Forces do on our behalf should be heralded. They are heroes and should be treated accordingly.

As the only novice rider to have been accepted to compete in the Mongol Derby (a 1000km horse race across Mongolia), I'm hoping to raise much needed awareness and cash for **Help for Heroes**.

The thought of this keeps me going every time I bounce off the ground as I learn to ride!

Above, from left: Will Kemble Clarkson, Jeremy Pemberton and Emily Morris-Lowe.

Nathan Reed **Everest Marathon 2009**

Help for Heroes is a hugely important cause to me.

I am a teacher, a historian and a patriotic guy, who believes that our soldiers and their sacrifices, both past and present, should be recognised by young and old alike, and that they should be supported.

So I wanted to do something to raise money for this worthy cause.

I love a challenge and had always thought I could run a pretty decent marathon. I had also always had an interest in Everest and a desire to trek to, at least, Base Camp. So, when I realised I could combine all three, it seemed like a fantastic opportunity.

I am not sure I realised how challenging it would be, but that is what I wanted!

Two weeks after leaving school, I joined the Junior Leaders Regiment Royal Artillery. After a year's training, I joined my adult unit at 47 Regiment, a Field Regiment (Guns) based at Thorney Island, near Emsworth in Hampshire. During the next 17 years of my career, I did various tours, of Northern Ireland, of Bosnia, of Afghanistan and finally one of Iraq, Op Telic 6 which ended in October 2005. On this tour I was promoted to Sergeant.

Six weeks after my return from theatre, I was involved in a near-fatal RTA. Driving in excess of 100mph I lost control of my car and ended up in some trees. I was rushed to hospital in a coma, with multiple injuries. The fact that I was twice the drink drive limit, may, ironically, have saved my life. The prognosis was that I wouldn't survive until the morning, and tests showed that I was brain dead (nothing new there!).

I spent the next two weeks in a coma, followed by a further three months in hospital. When I was discharged, I spent about a month at my parent unit before being admitted to the DMRC at Headley Court. I spent the next six months

there, learning how to walk properly, talk properly, eat and drink properly, and generally just getting to grips with not being able to do the same things that I used to be able to do.

Headley Court is an absolutely fantastic place. Everyone you speak to is an expert in one thing or another, and they gladly pass on their expertise to help you. I went there knowing nothing of my injuries; now, they have made me an expert on my own brain injury so that I am able to know why I think the way I do or say the things I do. By all the paramedics and surgeons/doctors who saved my life, I am humbled ... That people don't judge you but want to help you regardless, is remarkable.

I was adamant that I would be able to go back to working in the Army. To me, the Army wasn't a job, it was my way of life.

I didn't like being told that I was going to be Medically Discharged. But gradually I began to realise that I could barely look after myself, let alone a troop of soldiers. So I reluctantly agreed to accept the discharge.

The whole experience has taught me that, no matter how bad you think things are, no matter how sorry you're feeling for yourself, there really is always somebody a lot worse off than you. Headley Court really puts everything into perspective. Who cares about money or how big your house is or what car you drive? What matters is whether you have the feet and legs to play football with your kids, whether you have both arms to pick them up when they come out of school, and whether you know and recognise who your friends and family are.

I do not see myself as a hero – after all, my injury was the sole result of my own stupidity. There are other men and women out there who fit that description much better than I ever could. ▰

I served with the Household Cavalry. Five weeks into my stay in Helmand, on 1 August 2006, we were accompanying a Danish supply convoy. Taliban fighters suddenly started firing at us from high walls on either side of the road. The vehicle in front kept going and, as my Commander, sitting behind me, told me to reverse, a roadside bomb hit our armoured Scimitar and the back was blown off, killing my Commander and two others.

A rocket propelled grenade then struck the vehicle's engine, which exploded and engulfed me in flames. Jumping out of the vehicle I broke my arm, but I managed to pull off my body armour and helmet before rolling around in the sand to try to put out the flames. As I crawled for cover behind a wall, I was shot in my right leg.

I didn't feel it but I saw my leg fly out to one side. I thought I was going to die. I could only think of Michelle, my beloved fiancée. If I didn't get out of this, then I was letting her down.

My mates realised I was missing and risked their lives to rescue me. I was rushed back to Camp Bastion, and airlifted to hospital in the UK. I apparently 'died' three times on the long journey but each time was revived.

My father, Rob, called Michelle to tell her what had happened and they came together to Broomfield Hospital Burns Unit in Chelmsford, Essex, where I had been taken. I was covered from head to toe in bandages and my body had swelled up enormously. Michelle said, 'I didn't trust myself to speak so I just told you silently that I loved you and that you had to live.'

For the next three months, she sat at my bedside every day. She watched in anguish as I underwent 15 operations. Some were skin grafts using skin grown artificially as not enough of my own was available. With 70 per cent burns, my weakened body succumbed to infection and at one point my temperature soared to a life-threatening 43C° (110F°). Michelle was warned that, if I did regain consciousness, I could lose an arm and a leg.

After three months, I came round, and the first thing I saw was my loved ones. Michelle had plastered photographs all over my room.

Eventually I was transferred to Headley Court for rehabilitation, and I saw myself in the mirror for the first time. Just the two of us were there when Michelle held up the mirror for me. She said, 'If you turn into a recluse, you will no longer be you and I am walking out.'

I thought I looked so horrible I cried for an hour. I still felt like myself on the inside, I just didn't look like me on the outside. Michelle cried too and I told her I would understand if she didn't want to marry me. But she insisted I was still the man she loved.

Over the next year, she helped me on the slow and painful road to recovery. It wasn't easy having to be cared for, but the truth is, I'd never have made it without her.

We had set a date for our wedding and, a month after leaving hospital, I defied the doctors and walked a few steps. I was determined to walk down the aisle with Michelle, which I did in July 2008. I was the luckiest man alive!

I do not regret my time in the Army. I started going astray as a young teenager and decided instead to make something of my life. I am now thinking of doing motivational talks and am writing a book about my experiences.

What happened to me was just one of those things. There is no point in being bitter. ▉

I've always thought that it is important to journey through life, living it to the full and to make sure that you treat others as you would have them treat you. As C S Lewis said 'You are never too old to set a new goal or to dream a new dream.'

Towards the end of July 2005, after three months on Operations, working in and around Baghdad with a coalition Weapons Intelligence Unit known as CEXC, I came extremely close to death when I was very severely injured in an improvised explosive device explosion. As a result of the incident I lost my left leg above the knee, my left arm below the elbow and suffered extensive damage to my right leg, buttocks and back.

The four years following the incident in which I was injured have been the most challenging of my life. The very long period in hospital, even longer in rehabilitation and then, just as I was about to return home, losing my family through the separation and a subsequent divorce at the end of it, have been difficult. But throughout it all the thought of seeing my children, Tom and Toby, again has kept me going. They, and the fantastic people I have met during that time, all of the guys who have passed through Headley Court on their own journeys but maintained that unique military sense of humour and zest for life, and people such as Ross Kemp, who has done a fantastic job of portraying what the Armed Forces are experiencing on the ground in Afghanistan and who continues to be such a great supporter back home.

I've always admired the life and achievements of Sir Ernest Henry Shackleton CVO OBE, (15 February 1874 – 5 January 1922) a determined explorer and outstanding leader, who displayed so many of the attributes that are required of military officers.

The whole experience of the last four years has undoubtedly changed me: hopefully for the better. I think I appreciate my true friends and family more and I look for ways of giving back to the community. ■

> ❛I think there are two maxims I would pass on – that you should 'Be true to your work, your word, and your friends' (Henry David Thoreau) and to remember that 'The greatest glory in living lies not in never falling, but in rising every time we fall' (Nelson Mandela).❜

Opposite: Major Peter Norton with James May at the RHS Chelsea Flower Show 2009.

This page, clockwise from top left, Major Peter Norton with Sandi Toksvig, Lesley Joseph, Nancy Dell'Olio, Alison Steadman, Rolf Harris, members of 'The Feeling', and Jools Holland.

Opposite, clockwise from top left, with Philip Schofield, Laurence & Jackie Llewelyn-Bowen, Alan Titchmarsh, Will Young, Rosie, Lawrence Dallaglio & Mitzi Richards, Cheryl Howard and, centre, with Chelsea Pensioners.

All pictures taken at the RHS Chelsea Flower Show 2009.

Calum and Ollie Brown **TheThree Peaks Challenge**

Our names are Calum and Ollie and we are twin brothers aged twelve. We really want to raise money for a charity that means a lot to us. It is called **Help for Heroes** and it raises money to help our wounded servicemen and women. Every week we watch the news and it is so sad to see our soldiers getting seriously wounded or killed in Afghanistan. Then we all watched the Paras receiving their medals at Colchester and saw about a dozen soldiers who had been wounded, which was even more sad.

We both play rugby, and our local rugby club supports **Help for Heroes** as their special charity.

Our brother, Matt, is an Army Captain and has already served in Iraq. He is due to go to Afghanistan soon, so **Help for Heroes** is the obvious charity for our family to support.

We all decided that, as a family (Mum, Dad, Stacey – big sister, Matt and us) we will climb the three biggest mountains in Scotland, England and Wales – the Three Peaks Challenge. First we will be climbing Ben Nevis, the highest mountain of them all, in Scotland. Then we will climb Scafell Pike in England and finally Snowdon in Wales. The total height we will have to climb will be nearly 11,000 feet.

Mum and Dad have told us it will be the hardest thing we have ever done, so we have to put in lots of hard work to train for it. We want to climb these mountains over three days.

My name is Terry Byrne. I have been a Lance Corporal in 2 Para for roughly seven years and done four operational tours. In Afghanistan, I was a Section Commander in 7 Plt C Coy 2 Para.

After being out there for four months, on the 13 August in the early morning, I was leading a Company Patrol around FOB Gibraltar at 04:05. I stood on a pressure pad IED (Improvised Explosive Device). It blew me to the ground.

When I checked myself out, my leg was severely broken and twisted and my right hand was badly damaged. This later led to the amputation of my right leg below the knee and my right little finger.

As I started to recover in hospital, and later in rehab, I started to look at the Paralympics as they were doing 'Talent ID' days. My chosen sports were cycling and rowing... cycling because Britain was pretty awesome at this, and rowing because Sir Steve Redgrave was involved in it and I remember watching him as I was growing up. Anybody who can go that long, unbeaten, has a massive will to win and hugely strong character and I think this is needed to be a strong leader at soldiering or strong in sports, and I look up to that.

Meeting Sir Steve was awe-inspiring – what he has done in his career and what he has achieved! ▮

'We take our Forces for granted but over the last couple of years with the Help for Heroes campaign, hopefully, our Forces can see how proud we all are of them.

I feel very humbled that Terry looks up to me, when it is we who should be motivated by people such as him.'
Sir Steve Redgrave, CBE

I was injured on 12 June 2008, while commanding my Battle Group near a village we knew as 'Kats', 7km north of Musa Qaleh.

The troops were engaged in some feisty firefights as they made their way into Kats, but thankfully with no casualties. I sat with my Tac HQ on the fringes of the village, monitoring progress across the Battle Group.

We moved to some high ground to confirm reference points and other details. There was a long and intense burst of fire from over my left shoulder. One of the rounds entered through the back of my right thigh, shattered my femur and exited through the front. Luckily I was hit only once.

As the firefight continued a medic applied a tourniquet and dressings, improvised a splint from a tree branch and administered morphine. Then our MO arrived and took over. I remember clearly seeing him at one stage with a bone saw in his hand. Apparently my face revealed my thoughts but all he wanted to do was reduce the length of the splint!

At Camp Bastion I was operated on as soon as I arrived. Later I called home to tell Alison, my wife, what had happened, but, because my voice sounded odd, she thought I was a malicious caller and hung up! The following night I was flown to Birmingham and admitted to Selly Oak Hospital, where I spent five weeks receiving outstanding treatment and care. I had two further operations and discovered that I had lost about five centimetres of bone. After consultations at the Northern General Hospital in Sheffield I decided to have my damaged leg lengthened, rather than my good leg shortened. Four months later, after a series of setbacks and operations, both legs are the same length.

It has been a long haul and I'm not yet at the end. I will wear my Illizarov fixator until the new bone has set and will continue to attend Headley Court, whose fabulous staff will ensure that everything that can work does, for the foreseeable future. You need look no further than Headley Court for inspiration; the young men and women here, many of whom have suffered horrific, life-changing, injuries are relentlessly positive. When I have a bad day I need only to look at them to realise just how lucky I am.

I have always known that my amazing wife, Alison, is a strong lady, but her emotional strength this year has been remarkable. She has been a rock of support to me and to our daughters, Jenna and Clara. This whole episode has brought us even closer. And the children have been amazingly understanding too. It is not easy taking all this in at the ages of thirteen and eleven, yet they have coped brilliantly and add to the motivation to get fit again.

It has been an amazing time; not a journey I would have chosen to embark on but I am probably better for it. My horizons have broadened and I know now what is really important in life: life itself and the people you love. Added to that, I will always do my best for the amazing young men and women I have had the privilege to command and to share time with at Headley Court. ▓

Help for Heroes is a truly remarkable story. It moved rapidly from being an idea to becoming a national phenomenon. Clearly it was and is a worthy cause. But if it were nothing more than that, it surely would not have evoked the astonishing public response that we have seen. It has caught the imagination and touched the spirit of the nation to a most unusual degree. In part that is because it has reminded people that the men and women of the Armed Forces are acting on this nation's behalf; that their sacrifices are made in order to protect the people of this country and their interests. That is a unique commitment and it has called forth a correspondingly unique response. This book, portraying as it does the people of our Armed Forces, the challenges that some of them face when they return wounded from operations, and the work of **Help for Heroes** to support them in that struggle, serves both to underline and to strengthen the crucial link between military and public. It is a tribute to a group of men and women who do and bear much on our behalf, and to a charity that has achieved so much in nurturing and developing the connection between them and the society from which they spring and which they serve. I commend it to you.

My son, who is in the Parachute Regiment, returned from a six-month tour in Afghanistan in October 2008 and I went to see him and his colleagues receive their service medals at Colchester, presented by their Commander-in-Chief, His Royal Highness, the Prince of Wales. Ten of my son's friends and colleagues, who had lost limbs whilst in Afghanistan, were in wheelchairs to receive their medals. Seeing these wounded servicemen gave me the will and inspiration to 'do something' to help. Servicemen who are killed in action always make the headlines, whereas those who receive life-changing injuries are rarely mentioned. **Help for Heroes** are changing this. They do a fantastic job in aiding the rehabilitation of wounded military personnel and I decided that I would kayak around the coast of Britain to raise money to help them continue their valuable work.

It was whilst serving (for 22 years) in the Duke of Wellington's Regiment (now the 3 Yorks), that I gained my sea kayaking qualification in the early 1990s. Since then I have led several kayaking trips including crossing the English Channel to France, Northern Ireland to Scotland and back and a sea kayaking trip around the Outer Hebrides. I led a charity event in aid of the Bradford Football Stadium Fire Appeal, where members of my Battalion and I paddled 280 kilometres from the Guatemalan Border to Belize City. I have run sea kayaking courses for servicemen at the Joint Services Adventure Training Centre in Wales.

I set off from Blackpool Pier and paddled north, up the west coast to Fort William and the Caledonian Canal, then continued in a clockwise direction, returning to Blackpool Pier.

I used a Nordkapp Sea Kayak generously loaned by Valley Sea Kayaks, and had been training since March. I had good support from my friends, who got up early, usually on Sunday mornings (and sometimes during the week), to drive me to my training area, take photographs, shout encouragement, laugh at my misfortunes, and pick me up at the finish point, not to mention driving me home, so I could relax after the paddle! Ribby Hall Holiday Village gave me free membership to their state-of-the-art Fitness Centre, and here I could use the gym, have a swim and finish off in the sauna, to ease my aching muscles. I was also loaned a Marine Chartplotter by the GPS specialists, Garmin.

I arranged fundraising days, where an army of young volunteers agreed to 'bag pack' at the local supermarket, whilst I manned my **Help for Heroes** merchandise stall.

Local businesses have been very generous donating prizes and gift vouchers, which I am hoping to either auction or raffle at an end-of-event party, sometime later in 2009. ∎

My name is Mark Ormrod and I was a member of 40 Commando Royal Marines. I was seriously injured on a routine foot patrol on Christmas Eve 2007. I was part of an eight-man Section on a joint patrol with the rest of our Company, who were tasked to patrol a set route, as a show of force, as we had been confined to the FOB for several weeks due to lack of man power. It was a very basic and fairly short patrol and was going well up until the last leg when we were tasked to give cover to another Section returning to the safety of the FOB. The whole Section were on the high ground set into fire positions covering their arcs. I was one of the last to get into position to give cover and, as I took the last step before going to ground, I stood on and detonated an anti-personnel mine with a Chinese rocket attached. The blast tore off both my legs and my right arm; it caused various shrapnel wounds and burns and left a huge gash across the palm of my left hand. The blast was so big it left a crater eight feet deep and fifteen feet around. I had to have 28 pints of blood pumped through my body before I was stabilised.

After having my injured limbs amputated and being treated at Camp Bastion, I was flown back to the UK to Selly Oak Hospital, Birmingham, where I spent a week in Intensive Care and a further five weeks on the Burns and Plastics Ward, having further operations and recovering from my injuries and regaining my strength. Once I was deemed fit enough, I was transferred to Headley Court Rehabilitation Centre, where I was to begin my intense rehab programme and be fitted with prosthetic legs and a prosthetic arm.

Six months after arriving at Headley Court, I took part in a charity parachute jump to help raise money for the Forces Charity, SSAFA, who had funded the building of a £2 million mansion close to Headley Court for the families of injured service personnel to stay in when visiting their relatives. After that, my rehab continued and I continued to practise and get better, using my prosthetic limbs, with the intention of getting back to a normal life as soon as possible.

In October that same year, using my prosthetic limbs, I started on a graduated 'return to work' programme, aimed at building me up to return to a full-time job, and in the hope of continuing my career.

Now my time is split between working and continuing my rehab. Every Friday, I take a look back at the previous week and see what I have achieved and I set goals for the following week. Life has been very hard since my accident and I have had to adapt as best I can to try and lead as normal a life as possible... and it is very possible. I'm not the kind of person to sit back and feel sorry for myself. I just look at what has happened to me as another challenge in life and one that I plan to tackle like I would any other. ▮

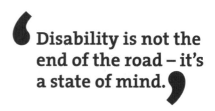

Disability is not the end of the road – it's a state of mind.

Opposite: Mark Ormrod & wife Becky

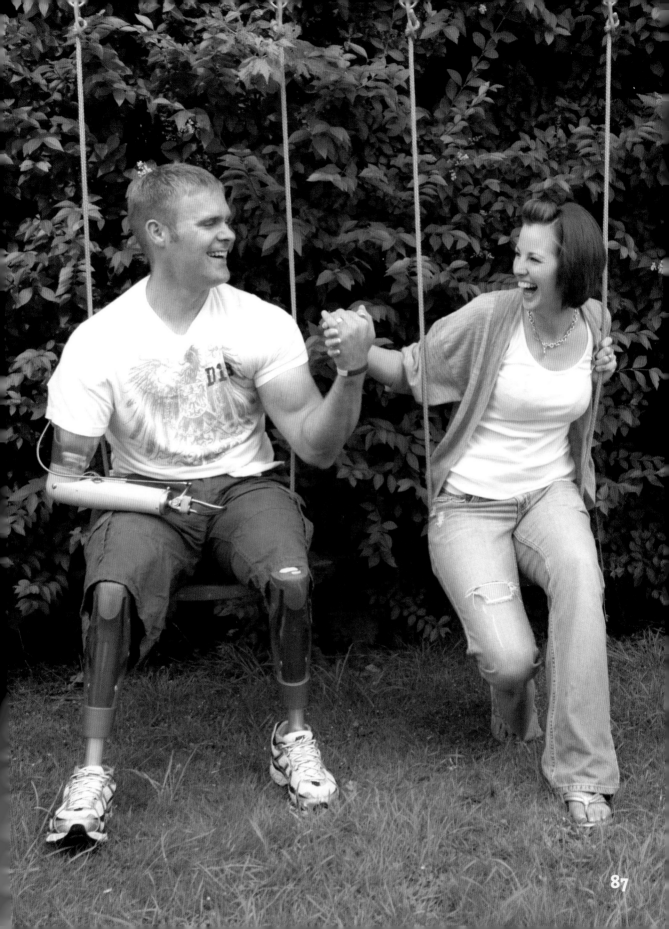

The accident happened on the 5 February 2007. It was a Monday morning and me and my girlfriend at the time were out the house at about 06:30 to meet my colleague at a junction on the M5 at 07:00 to give me a lift down the line to Dartmoor, to go on a two-week excercise with our company. Unfortunately, we didn't make the junction and we crashed just outside my home town. The car rolled down an embankment and came to rest upside down. My 'ex' was free from the car but I was trapped. Finally I was cut from the car and taken to Worcester Royal Infirmary where I was in Intensive Care for about three days. On the Thursday lunchtime, I was airlifted to Oswestry (a specialist spinal injuries unit), where I stayed for, roughly, two and a half months – mending. The team there are amazing people to say the least. They saved my life and the lives of many more people in my situation, and they deserve great praise.

For the first two weeks I was at Oswestry, I was 'under observation'. I then had six weeks bedrest – which was unbearable. Six weeks of lying on your back, eating, washing, toileting and, above all else, the time to think about your new life and everything that goes with it. The remaining time was spent rehabilitating gently, whilst the bones fixed fully (I broke L1, T8, T9 and spinal cord damage at T10). When I was released, I was sent down to the Military Rehab Centre at Headley Court for about a month. After that, I moved into my mum's, which, to say the least, wasn't ideal. My mum lives in a three-storey terrace house, with steps up to the front and back. Kindly, my brother, my dad and a good friend made the back of the house wheelchair-accessible, but, for about six months, I made my way up to the toilet and my bedroom, which were on the first floor, on my backside, shimmying up the stairs. This was good

in a way, because it gave me my upper-body strength back. I finally found a bungalow in Aston Somerville near Broadway which is great and easier than climbing stairs! (Although I still visit my mum for Sunday roasts!)

Going back to the six weeks of bed-rest... the time spent there, and the first year and a half after the accident, was the worst time of my life. It's very hard even to begin to think about the implications and the sheer loss of it all – going from being a super-fit, young, Royal Marines Commando to being a cripple is tough... and sometimes overwhelming, reducing me to tears on a few occasions. There are so many things to think about, how it will affect my future, my job, my quality of life, girlfriends, sex, my super-bike, fitness, life expectancy, kids, day-to-day jobs and tasks such as DIY, helping mum and dad, etc etc. You start to question your manhood and how it detracts from that, ask yourself how can I fend for myself? How do I protect those close to me? Do they need to protect me now? How do people see me? All of these subjects still cause frustration, but not as much. You think about suicide on many occasions... how to do it? What would it be like for those I left? A massive list of things runs through your head and, with six weeks' bed rest, you watch every minute on that clock ticking by.

During this time there was no one that really inspired me or spurred me on. This was a very personal journey and, even if there had been anyone, I would have been in too much of a bad mood even to listen to what they had to say.

As you would imagine, something like this turns you very angry and builds a lot of tension

Opposite: Mike Miller-Smith (left), Mike Owen (behind) and Arthur Williams (right)

'Flying is an amazing tool to help disabled people rehabilitate through the realisation that they can still achieve incredible things.

Flying is an achievement for anybody, and a disabled person might think 'If I could fly, maybe I could work again, or start a family, or drive a car, or achieve other everyday goals'.'

Mike Miller-Smith, Chief Executive of BDFA

inside that often gets vented on those closest to you, which at the time was my mum. I found that being a Marine made me even more frustrated than others and I have seen many anger management people up until only recently, as the anger is the hardest thing to shake off. I feel I still have a much shorter fuse now, even two years after the injury.

Acceptance takes a long time – at least a year, just to accept the most obvious of things like the fact you haven't got abdominal stability or the ability to sit up unaided for a while. You think you can just heal and go home. 'OK, I might need a wheelchair but yeah, no problem!' Then, accepting that people want to help without snapping at them. And dealing with the way people seem to be patronising you, but you have to tell yourself 'Of course they don't know what you can and can't do Arthur, they just don't want to see you struggle'. So you let them help, although you have to draw the line sometimes.

So that brings us up to date, pretty much. Life now is great. I'm back on track, back to my old self, new house, car, girlfriend, future, and now

learning to fly with scope for being a pilot for a career. I look at my life and put the old and the new on a set of scales, trying to balance out the old with the new. On one hand I have my old life as a Royal Marine, girlfriend, super-bike, living at my mum's, and my fitness; and, on the other hand, now I have my own house, an accepting and supportive girlfriend (who is probably my only inspiration), car, fitness, ex-Royal Marine and training to fly.

And now I think I can honestly say that my new life is better than the old, and that makes me feel great with an inner comfort I have been struggling desperately to find for so long. ▮

‘ **Arthur is an exceptional student and obviously very capable; his disability is no barrier for him.** ’
Mike Owen,
Flying Instructor, BDFA Lasham

I was in Incaman, North Sangin, in Afghanistan on 7 May 2009. We went out on reconnaissance, to find a drop zone for a helicopter drop and to look for 'well sites' for the locals. I was told later five vehicles were in front of us but, as we came around a bit of a hill in a Jackal Vehicle, we hit a mine. My driver sadly died immediately and the gunner and I were flung from the vehicle. The Americans came and picked us up and took us back to Bastion. I can still only remember four days before the incident and two weeks after when I woke up in Selly Oak Hospital and my dad was saying 'You are in the UK and fine, but you've been in an accident'. I had a head injury and lung damage. I arrived here at Headley Court on 3 June. I am so grateful for the treatment I have received from everyone but especially from my own guys who treated me when the explosion happened. Their care was second to none! ▮

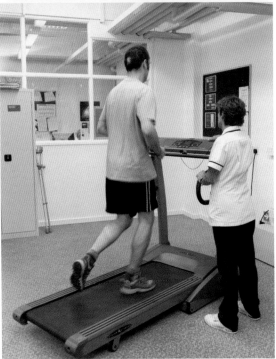

It's been an hour. The streets are very quiet. Something is just not right. It feels hostile, as if something is going to happen. We stop next to a local shop; we have spoken to the shopkeeper once before. He was very nice and talkative, but this time he won't talk to us.

As we make our way back through the city, I notice the football stadium. It's nothing like ours back home. It's been blown to bits. I shout out, "Oh look! There's Villa Park!" Lee just laughs as he's a Birmingham fan. John's not happy as he's a Villa fan. The banter is good between us.

The roads are covered in litter and rubble. There are no kids around, which is strange; it's very quiet. I sat thinking about my first tour. I was a young 17-year-old, just fresh from school. I was nervous, anticipating the worst back then. I have twelve years' experience now, but complacency never comes into it. We've trained hard for 18 months for this tour.

I hit the railway line at about 40mph. I hear a loud explosion, then a second one. I lose control of the Land Rover. I try to brake. The gap between the explosions seems like an eternity but, after the first, everything slows down. I feel excruciating pain in my left arm, and my right arm is numb. My right leg is very painful. I'm trying desperately hard to stop the vehicle. We are bouncing all over the place and hit a wall. I am screaming at John but he's not responding. I try to lift my left arm to grab him but it's not moving. I know my right arm isn't there any more. The vehicle has stopped. Nick drags me out of the vehicle and lays me on the dry mud. I stop screaming. Everything has stopped being in slow motion; time has caught up with itself.

I can't breathe. I say, 'Can someone open my body armour? Is John ok? Is he alive?'

I'm shouting 'Is John OK? Is he alive?'

'John is breathing', says someone. I am relieved, desperately hoping he is OK.

I open my eyes. I look up to see Stevie looking at me. He asks 'Where is your arm?'

'In the Land Rover somewhere, go get it, stick it back on.'

We both start laughing. I'm laughing in pain, the pain is agonising. I don't know how long has passed; I think only a few minutes. It seems longer.

The QRF and the ambulance arrive. It seems like an eternity. I am put into the ambulance, with John.

It is very uncomfortable in the ambulance, bouncing all over the place; the roads in Iraq are not the best. I am on the right hand side of the ambulance. My arm is hitting the side. The pain is unbelievable. I look over to John. I notice the medics doing CPR on him. I say, 'He was breathing! What are you doing? Is he OK?' I get no answer.

It's only a short journey back to base. It's very hot and sticky in the ambulance. It stops. I feel the hot air on my face. I am moved off the stretcher on to a bed and they start cutting my combats off.

I think I'm dead; I'm not in my body any more. I'm not in any pain, it feels nice. I don't know

where I am. I see lots of different colours, pinks, blues, like I'm tripping. There is a nice breeze on my body keeping me cool. It's beautiful. I wake up. I don't know where I am. I'm scared. There are four to five nurses around me. I don't recognise any of them.

'Where am I?' I ask.

'Shaibah Hospital.'

'Is John here?'

'Who is John? Don't know a John.'

'Sergeant Jones.'

The darkest moments of our lives are not to be buried or forgotten. They are a memory to be called upon for inspiration to remind us of our capacity to overcome the intolerable. After seven operations, two years of anxiety, depression and guilt, you start to look at life differently. I used to live life to be happy; now I'm happy to be alive, to see my kids grow up. Life will knock you down every time if you let it; it's how you get back up that counts. I look forward to the new challenges in my life, the new career that awaits me. ■

The idea for the trip started off as an interesting and different way of celebrating my friend Jack's 21st birthday. For some time, we had both been keen to do a long car journey into Europe, and we decided this was our best opportunity, setting our sights on Germany and the Nürburgring race track in the hope of having a go at a few laps of the circuit.

Our first task was deciding on a car. Jack, having always been a fan of classic cars, started looking at a few different possibilities. Luck came to us in the form of a 1968 Jaguar Mk2 and we were quick to decide that this was the car for the trip, despite the extensive work that needed doing to get it back on the road again.

To make the trip even more worthwhile, we came up with the great idea of trying to raise some money for charity. We chose **Help for Heroes**, a brilliant charity that we both fully support.

We got stuck straight into working on the Jaguar and, with support from some very helpful sponsors, Jag Breakers (www.jagbreakers.org), SNG Barratt (www.sngbarratt.com), Bucks University (www.bucks.ac.uk), and Man batteries (www.manbat.com) we had it up and running and ready for the long trip that was ahead of us.

Nigel Butler **From John O'Groats to Lands End**

We are a team of three from Stourbridge: my eldest son, Gareth, our friend Graham Dalby and myself. We decided to enter my 1967 Morris Minor in the JOGLE, an endurance event which requires you to drive from John O'Groats to Land's End, inside 24 hours, to raise money for the charity **Help for Heroes**.

The weather throughout the trip was mixed, sunny, sea mist, fog inland and drizzle. It was due to the drizzle that we had our only hair-raising moment when, going round a sharp left-hand hairpin, the rear wheel slipped on a wet manhole cover leaving us fishtailing down the road.

At our only checkpoint at Oldbury, we found we had only one headlight, and further down the M5 we had a flat battery, but after one push start we were on our way.

We arrived at Land's End in bright sunshine, having covered the 874 miles in 21 hours and 50 minutes. All funds raised from this event and from car shows throughout the year will go to **Help for Heroes**, in memory of my late uncle, a veteran of D-Day (who would have taken part in this trip) and for my niece, serving in the RAF, who is being posted to Afghanistan in 2009. ■

Corporal Andy Pennock 204 Signal Squadron

I had a lower back injury in June 2008 which needed an operation, now having lots of physio and time in the gym! Hopefully I will be fully fit to go on Op-Herrick in 2010. ■

Roy Kendall

After 17 years in the Royal Engineers and three separate stays in two different military hospitals, I set up a company (www.top-of-the-range.co.uk) in 1993 which supplies every regiment in the Army, Royal Marines, Royal Navy and RAF. We also design and manufacture our own range of specialist equipment and clothing.

We continue successfully today as the sole European distributor for the complete Bugout Range, the UK distributor for Under Armour Tactical, and the military agent for Power Traveller. We also supply items from next-to-skin to outerwear, luggage and accessories. All items have been designed and checked for suitability and we have had items on top of the world on Everest and across the Atlantic with Peter Bray.

We are very proud of our link with the military and are extremely pleased to be associated with **Help for Heroes**.

Good luck, stay safe and thank you. ■

In September 2005 I joined the Honourable Artillery Company, my local TA Regiment, where I began a gruelling six-month Recruits' Course. In March 2006 I passed the course and was selected to start training for a specialist role as an 'STA (Surveillance and Target Acquisition) Patrol Soldier' which would enable me to gain entry into one of the three combat-ready Sabre Squadrons.

In May 2007, with my employer's blessing, I began a two-year sabbatical from my civilian life as an investment consultant and mobilised into full-time soldiering. At Marne Barracks, Catterick, I was attached to the HAC's regular equivalent, 4/73 Special OP Battery Royal Artillery. Here I spent the best part of five months training full-time with the battery, learning new skills and enhancing old skills.

On the 3 October 2007 I deployed to Afghanistan with A troop 4/73 BTY. Within two weeks of arrival in theatre we took up our role as the Bridge Reconnaissance Force (BRF). Essentially, we were the Bridge Commanders' eyes on the ground.

After two months of successful operations, our luck ran out when a vehicle in my patrol struck a mine, instantly killing the top cover and injuring the driver and vehicle commander. This was a bitter blow for the BRF but an even bigger blow for me, as the soldier killed was a very close friend who had started training with me right from the beginning of my army career in the HAC. With his death temporarily put to one side, we remained focused on our job and, in early December 2007, we were instrumental in the overturn of power from the Taliban to coalition forces of Musa Qala (MQ) district.

After spending over 100 days without returning to camp, which included being out for both Christmas and New Year, 20 January 2008 is a date that I will never forget. On the return leg, my vehicle struck a mine under the front left wheel, instantly turning the vehicle through 180 degrees and injuring all three of us who were in it. My top cover flew out of his turret breaking his arm, my Commander broke both of his shins and I, the driver, had fractured my knee. We were carried into another vehicle and driven up to meet a helicopter but we hit another mine. This time the mine struck under the front right wheel. The driver died instantly. I was sitting next to the driver in the Commander's seat and was thrown some 20 metres out of the vehicle, whilst the other two, who were also in the previous mine strike, plus an additional medic, were trapped in the vehicle, now on its side in flames. The next thing I remember is having water poured on my face to wash off the oil and shrapnel and to wake me up. Clearly we were in a mine field, so this time we were all stretchered and carried by foot to the helicopter.

Three days later I found myself back in the UK, receiving treatment for minor shrapnel wounds and multiple fractures to my right knee. I began a series of rehabilitation courses at DMRC Headley Court where I find myself today, twelve months on, still receiving treatment on my knee. I am yet to return to my civilian job.

However I am keeping myself extremely busy by helping to raise money for **Help for Heroes**. In September 2008, two friends and I organised a rugby match held at Twickenham.

I have also completed a cycle ride from Portsmouth to Paris. ◼

Opposite: Adam Cocks with Mayor of London Boris Johnson

I have been a Consultant for five years in Emergency Medicine in the Army or, as it is now called, the Defence Medical Services. I have deployed to Iraq on four occasions, beginning with the ground war in 2003 as a specialist registrar with one of the dressing stations. Since then I have deployed to Iraq on three further occasions and, in early summer 2008, I deployed on OP Herrick to Camp Bastion. There, I was Consultant in the Emergency Department and went out on the Medical Emergency Response Team on board a Chinook to pick up casualties from the point of wounding. When not deployed, I work in Queen Alexandra Hospital in Portsmouth as part of MDHU (Ministry of Defence Hospital Unit) Portsmouth. I have worked there for seven years.

I decided to run the London Marathon in 2009 for **Help for Heroes**. I began training in earnest before Christmas. It is not easy to find time for training with a busy job, long commute and a young family,

but there is no option but to put in the miles.

The race itself started well. It was great to start with another **Help for Heroes** runner and I passed the final minutes before the start chatting to him. The crowds were great. Having my name on my T shirt helped, as lots of people shout out and it does keep you going. There were also a lot of people who recognised the charity and shouted out in support for that. The day was certainly hot and I managed to keep going well to about 21 miles. It was great to see the other **Help for Heroes** runners, especially the one carrying a bergen and wearing combats!

After 21 miles it was very hard and I walked and jogged from that point on. The three things that definitely kept me going were the thought of the money I was raising and the fact that it was for the injured, who put up with far worse hardships than my 26 miles; and also the other **Help for Heroes** runners, who exhorted me to keep going as they ran past me! ■

Opposite: Simon Hunter and Bryan Reynolds – in white T shirts, and (left) Guardsmen from the 1st Battalion Grenadier Guards welcome Simon and Bryan to Wellington Barracks at the end of the 2009 London Marathon.

Commissioned in 2004, I currently work at HQ Joint Medical Command.

Prior to my current posting in April 2009, I worked at 3 Medical Regiment as a Squadron Second-in-Command for 12 Squadron. As a Squadron, we deployed on Op TELIC 12 to last year, returning in December 2008. Although it was a very quiet and successful tour in terms of casualties, my previous deployment on TELIC 7 was not.

Whilst we were in the UK, the Medical Group in which I was part of the Close Support Squadron, regularly held fundraising events in order to raise money for charity. The majority of the money raised went to **Help for Heroes**. It was then that I decided to run the London Marathon in support of **Help for Heroes**.

I am only 27 but I know several personnel who have been killed whilst on Operations, and even more people who have been seriously injured. It is fantastic the amount of money that has been raised by **Help for Heroes** to support injured servicemen and women, especially as the charity was set up by only two individuals.

I plan to have a full career in the Army and in the back of my mind I always keep the thought that, one day, I may need support from **Help for Heroes** myself, to restore me to good health as the result of an incident whilst on tour.

When so many young soldiers are selflessly putting their lives in danger, I felt that the least I could do was to help raise some money by running the Flora London Marathon. My cousin is in Afghanistan now, along with many friends of mine. Whilst, of course, I hope they do not get injured, if they do, at least I shall be able to say that I have helped to contribute, and I will continue to do so. ■

'It was truly inspirational to witness the end of Major Phil Packer's marathon, we felt privileged to be there and to meet with so many supporters including Sir Steve Redgrave.'

From left: Sapper Greg Stevenson, Marine Aaron Moon, L/Cpl Matthew O'Neill and Marine Andy Grant, at back (on the right of Sir Steve Redgrave) Private Dave Triplow.

At the end of November 1994, at the age of 22, whilst coming back from a job interview, I crashed my car (a 1963 MGB Roadster) into an oak tree near my parent's home in Yorkshire, where I was living since being medically discharged from the RMA, Sandhurst, four months previously.

After a six month stay in hospital I ended up losing my left leg below the knee, having my right ankle rebuilt, my head and face completely reconstructed and various other injuries patched up. I left hospital with no job, no leg, no income and no idea what I was going to do for the rest of my life, as all I had ever focused on, since the age of seven, was trying to make a career in flying and playing rugby union.

I got a job and moved to London, where I found it was easier not to go to the gym as it was such a hassle. At the same time I had to have two operations on my stump which meant I couldn't walk for months and so I ended up putting on a lot, and I mean a lot, of weight.

My girlfriend (now my wife), realising I needed to do some sport, suggested we try skiing as she had skied before she met me. We discovered that the BSCD, now Disability Snowsport UK, ran regular evenings throughout the year to teach the disabled to ski. From the first moment I put on skis, I loved it. Our honeymoon was spent in Winter Park, Colorado, home of the National Sports Centre for the Disabled (NSCD), an amazing and inspirational place.

With the total support of the NSCD, I went, in just over six weeks on snow, from complete beginner to being allowed to train with the Winter Park Race Squad, many of whom are competing in the Winter Olympics. This inspired me to go on a dramatic diet where I lost 50kgs in five months and started a proper exercise regime again.

In September 2007, I heard about **Help for Heroes** and having friends and family who served and are serving, thought what a great idea it was. I really wanted to do all I could to help, particularly as I understood how difficult it can be after losing a limb. I was especially interested in the Bike Ride although I hadn't cycled properly since losing my leg, but it was the best reason to make me get on my bike again. I ended up being adopted by 'Team Marine', and the Big Battlefield Bike Ride was one of the best weeks of my life. So much so, that we decided to do it again in 2009.

In the future, I am hoping to build upon all this and do much more with our wounded and, particularly, the amputees. Eventually, I would like to do this full-time, on the snow.

I appreciate what it's like to lose a limb in your prime and how hard it is, both mentally and physically, to recover and to rebuild one's life. Losing a limb is life-changing but I promise that your life is *not* over as a result. It's not about one door closing and another one opening; it's more like most of your old doors disappearing and a whole new set appearing that just weren't there before. Some of those may even be more appealing than the doors that disappeared.

The experiences that I have had and the amazing people that I have met as a result of my amputation have meant I have had so much fun since losing my leg that I could almost recommend it to anyone! ▓

My name is Darren Fuller. I am 32 years old and have been in the Parachute Regiment since 1994, most of the time with 2 Para but I have recently been posted to 4 Para for two years as a permanent Staff Instructor. I have been on eleven operational tours, including Northern Ireland, Macedonia, Iraq and Afghanistan. My whole time so far in the Army has been great, both pre- and post-injury.

On 26 March 2008, I deployed to Afghan on my second tour, as a Mortar Section Commander. After a week of mandatory training and live firing in Camp Bastion, I flew into the FOB with the rest of 2 Para D Company's advance party. Later we were joined by the rest of the company in Kajaki.

Early one morning, I took my men down to the mortar line and watched as D Company left on our first patrol. About an hour later, we were given our first fire mission which was to create a smoke screen as a deception, to make the enemy think the blokes were approaching them from a different direction. This was a success. Over the next 20 minutes or so there was increased activity by the enemy and everyone knew it was only a matter of time before it all kicked off.

Another smoke mission was sent for and we started to fire. Halfway through the number 2 barrel had a misfire, in other words the bomb was placed in the barrel but failed to go off. At this point the no 1 and no 3 barrels continued firing whilst we dealt with the misfire drill which we all knew inside out. Misfires are quite common. However little did I know that this misfire wouldn't end up in the normal way. There was a loud bang. I dropped to one knee with my ears ringing and my vision blurred. After a few seconds the ringing in my ears had dulled. I looked at my right arm and I realised it wasn't there any more. Somehow, as we were clearing

the misfire, it had gone off and ripped my right arm off. The blood was going everywhere and I knew this was serious and I would be getting casevaced back home. I was gutted, as I'd trained hard for this tour and wanted to complete it looking after myself and my men. I suppose you could say the thought of whether I would live or die did pop into my head at some point, but all I could think about was whether I would get to see my seven-year old son, Adam, and my fiancée, Annmarie, again. Luckily my blokes on the mortar line and another lad from 2 Para Anti Tanks, Lieutenant Corporal Nuth, to whom I will be eternally grateful, were beside me in seconds applying First Aid. If it had not been for these men and their quick reactions and medical skills, Lt Cpl Nuth in particular, I would have lost more of my right arm than I already had.

After an operation at a Dutch field hospital in Helmand Province the reality kicked in that my arm was gone. But I was alive.

Two days later I was flown back to Selly Oak Hospital, where I stayed for four weeks having another couple of operations and lots of antibiotics. After that I went to Headley Court, where I got my new prosthetic arm and began to put my life back together. My time at Headley was great and the treatment I received there was outstanding. I owe them a lot.

All the support and rehabilitation enabled me to return to work only five months after my injury. It also enabled me to complete the Band of Brothers Bike Ride for **Help for Heroes**, which entailed riding 350 miles in five days, just a year and a month after my injury.

To all who have supported me, especially Selly Oak Hospital, Headley Court, my Battalion 2 Para, my family and friends, my son Adam and my fiancée Annmarie, *thank you*. I won't forget it. ▩

My inspiration for organising this sponsored ride is that, as a palliative care nurse looking after people with cancer and other life-limiting illnesses, I see so much suffering, both from patients and their relatives, and I have looked after quite a few servicemen and women at the hospice over the last fourteen years.

My friend and colleague, Julie Lee, has three sons in the Army, whose careers I have followed closely. These three boys have become my focus and my reason for wanting to support all the servicemen and women who have laid their lives on the line for us.

It was while talking to Julie about her sons' experiences, that I decided to try and support our Armed Forces in some way. When I spoke to the helpers at the stables they were very keen and excited to do something too, and the idea of the sponsored ride was born. When I asked my 'helpers' why they were going to do this ride in support of our servicemen and women, these were their replies:

'So that the heroes can get help from the doctors and get what they need' – Katie aged nine.

'We want to raise money for **Help for Heroes** so that we can give something in return to the soldiers who have fought for our country' – Ellie aged fifteen and Phoebe aged eleven.

'So that we can have a water fight afterwards!' – Ross aged fourteen.

'So we can get dressed up and have a good time' – Olivia aged eight.

'For a laugh and to give the money to the soldiers' – Maisie aged eight.

'For dressing up and to help the charity' – Molly aged twelve. ▧

Private Christopher Chell Royal Army Medical Corps **Sponsored Tattoo**

I joined the Army in November 2000. I started my career in the Infantry with the Devon and Dorsets (now 1 Rifles).

My first posting was in Hounslow, Middlesex, where I joined C Company.

In 2002 – 2004, I did my first tour of Northern Ireland. Whilst there, I went to D Support and became a mortar-man.

In 2004, I became a Regimental Medical Assistant and, in April 2006, I served a seven-month tour in Iraq. Whilst there, I worked in the Regimental Aid Post. It was then that I decided to transfer to the Royal Army Medical Corps.

In 2007 I transferred to the Corps and am now a Combat Medical Technician with 22 Field Hospital, Aldershot.

The reason I decided to do this sponsored tattoo of the **Help for Heroes** medal, is that I have seen the aftermath of Iraq and Afghanistan. Sadly, while in Iraq, a friend of mine did lose his life and another was wounded.

Obviously, it felt painful having the tattoo done, but it was nothing compared to the pain that the guys felt through their injuries and that the families of the lost ones are feeling every day. ■

Tattoo carried out by Kevin Clark at *Grin'n'Bare It*, Farnborough.

Carried off a Puma after been blown up in Iraq 2004 (fractured skull)

On 9 February 2008, the Commando Reconnaissance Force, from 40 Commando Royal Marines was tasked with a Close Target Recce (CTR) of a suspected Taliban bomb-making factory.

We entered the target compound from the west through a gap in the perimeter wall. We were moving very silently using hand signals for communication. Our job was to gather evidence and extract covertly so our intelligence guys back at the FOB could determine exactly what the compound was used for. We gathered up a number of electrical items including batteries, circuit boards and wiring. We also found large quantities of fertiliser which was known to be used as an explosive.

On patrolling around to the front of the compound I took the lead. I patrolled through a small garden with the other three lads following behind. When I got to the middle of the garden I felt a tension around my legs. I knew what it was straight away and my heart sank. Upon looking down I heard the distinctive noise of a fly-off lever being released and then saw a grenade taped to a wooden stake in the ground fall in front of me. Two of the guys were directly behind me and I realised we were all going to get seriously injured. I only had a split second to decide what to do. I shouted 'grenade, take cover' and lay down next to the grenade with my daysack and body armour pointing towards it to provide a barrier. I brought my knees up and

tilted my head back to provide cover for the back of my neck, gritted my teeth and waited for the inevitable. Time seemed to go by slowly and I started to wonder if I had seen a rock rather than a grenade...

I remember seeing plumes of orange sparks, smoke, debris and dust. My ears were ringing and my nose streaming with blood. Pieces of my kit were later found over 50 metres away in other compounds. The force of the explosion blew me about a metre and it felt like someone had swung a baseball bat at my back several times. The team medic quickly gave me a head to toe before the lads got me to my feet. My Corporal had a small piece of shrapnel hit his nose but apart from that and the small injuries I had we were thankfully fine.

I lay up in a ditch with the company medic and waited for a couple of hours until people were seen near the compounds, a couple of the sections went in and arrested a number of people and tactical questioners went about their business. From the ditch I was in with a few E Coy guys and the medic nothing much seemed to be happening until the medic spotted someone across the river with an AK47. He was about 400m away so a decent distance and not the easiest of shots to take and hit first time, especially with him moving around. We observed for a while as he wasn't posing a threat at the time and rules of engagement stopped us opening fire. This gave me time though to adjust my sights and build a stable and calm firing position so I was 100 per cent ready if I could get a shot off. No more than a

In Iraq, 2004

minute or two later, the Taliban fighter lifted his weapon in our direction sealing his fate. He knew we were in the area but I doubt he knew where and how close and was probably concentrating his efforts on the arresting sections at the compounds we were in earlier. I fired two or three rounds and the man dropped to his knees scurrying to hide behind a bush. About five of us opened up on the bush and the fighter wasn't seen again.

When we completed the patrol I went to see the Doc who checked me out, and apart from concussion, bleeding nose, perforated ear drums, bruises etc, I wasn't too bad. I did get taken back on Chinook to Camp Bastion the following day however to get fully checked out.

Upon returning to the UK at the end of the tour the story leaked to a Sunday Times reporter who was in Helmand at the time. It was announced I was to receive the George Cross which was presented by Her Majesty The Queen at Buckingham Palace in October 2008. Everyone calls me a hero for what I've done but I accepted that things like that could happen when I joined the Royal Marines and it's all part of the job. My theory is anyone who has the balls to deploy to an operational theatre and serve their country is a hero.

I have undertaken six-and-a-half years serving in the regular Royal Marines and two years as a reservist. My full-time career now is as a director of Pinnacle Risk Management. I am still active in the Royal Marines Reserve and take a very active part in raising money for charities. The photograph above shows me in a **Help for Heroes** rugby match between the Royal Marines and Yardley and District Rugby Club. ◼

Buckingham Palace, July 2008

'**Help for Heroes** is a phenomenon. Of course it recognises the achievements of the remarkable people who make up our Armed Forces and their selfless sacrifice. But more widely it satisfies the desire of people throughout the country to salute and pay tribute to that sacrifice. As such it epitomises two significant British instincts: service and the recognition of service. The two enjoy an inseparable bond. Let us hope that condition endures, because it is fundamental to the moral well-being of our Armed Forces and the country they serve. '

Harry Long

I was a Captain in the Army with the 1st Battalion The Royal Green Jackets and, in January 2006, I was paralysed from the chest down in a mountain training exercise.

Having completed Sandhurst in 2002, I joined the Royal Green Jackets in Weeton Barracks on the outskirts of Blackpool. Like all Regiments in the post 9/11 period, we were constantly active with training and operational commitments, so much so that I once worked out I had spent eight weeks in camp in my first eighteen months with the Battalion. In that time, operations had taken us to Iraq and Northern Ireland.

At the end of 2004 I was posted to the Army Training Regiment at Pirbright, where I took up a training post instructing Phase 1 recruits. For the first time since joining the Army, this position gave eighteen months' stability and Abbie and I were married in the summer of 2005. Having been seeing one another since just before I joined the Army, like many other military relationships, Abbie had weathered a great deal of separation and uncertainty. However, Pirbright gave us the opportunity for our first home together and the chance of a 'normal' life.

However, in January 2006, *la dolce vita* took a bit of a swerve, as did I, when I fell from a ledge in a night-time mountain training exercise. The fall broke my neck and back and left me paralysed from the mid-chest down.

After spending five months in the NHS system, I was transferred to Headley Court for a further two months of rehabilitation and physiotherapy. Returning to the military system, and, more importantly, a sense of humour, was a fantastic feeling. Having been in a spinal unit surrounded by people with similar injuries to my own, it was humbling and intriguing to be introduced to the variety and extremities of injuries at Headley Court. Seeing others' coping mechanisms and being a part of the dark humour and camaraderie of the place went a long way to rationalising my own injuries.

On leaving Headley Court, Abbie and I moved to the Bristol area for a fresh start, where we continue to live and work. We became aware of **Help for Heroes** soon after it was founded and we enlisted in the inaugural bike ride. However, a last minute return to hospital meant I was, unfortunately, not able to participate. ▪

'Epic Greenland' was conceived by Margaret Bowling in late 2008 and was carried out by Niall McCann and Murray Smith. Margaret had put together a team of like-minded individuals with the aim of completing great challenges in adventuring.

Niall and Murray spent one week training in East Greenland with Marine Pete Bird before taking the chopper flight to the drop-off point.

The crossing took 24 days, during which Niall and Murray skied 550km across the Greenland icecap, climbed from sea level to an altitude of 2500m, endured temperatures inside their tent of below 25 (our thermometer only reads Lo after 25; one night it read Lo for over five hours, inside the tent!), and endured a wind chill factor while skiing of 35, in 17 ambient temperatures plus gale force 8 winds.

Murray suffered snow blindness for three days, put his leg down a concealed crevasse and had to walk out the final 72km after all our spare ski bindings perished. Niall has some minor frostbite on his fingertips.

Both of us suffered frightful blisters after our Marines issue boots lost all of their cushioning three weeks into the expedition. Both of us still had numb toes, nearly two weeks after having arrived in Kangerlussuaq!

We ate 6000 cal per day, skied for up to twelve hours in a day and skied over 38km on one day.

We wanted to raise money for **Help for Heroes** to help enable our wounded servicemen and women to live out their dreams of completing adventurous challenges such as ours.

We hope that we can inspire even one person to get out there and follow his or her ambition to challenge themselves in extreme environments. ▓

Opposite: Murray Smith, Margaret Bowling and Niall McCann, with Marine Pete Bird (kneeling).

S/Sgt Ryan Tolley, CSM Chris Smith, S/Sgt Shaun Haywood and S/Sgt Benn Cartwright,
Warwickshire & West Midlands (South Sector) Bravo Company.

We came up with this idea when we were trying to think how we could raise money for the charity **Help for Heroes**, because we wanted to aid the wounded soldiers who are out of action due to medical difficulties and disabilities.

We then decided, after a lot of thinking, that we wanted to do something big, so then one member of the group decided to do the 100 Mile Walk. The reason was that we thought this would be very demanding on us but would raise a lot of money.

The route:

Day 1   Shrewsbury to Ludlow
Day 2   Ludlow to Redditch via Kidderminster
Day 3   Redditch to Coventry via Warwick
Day 4   Coventry to Nuneaton
Day 5   Nuneaton to Bramcote Barracks

We also have a strong link with the charity, being serving members of the Army Cadet Force.

The Army Cadet Force (ACF) is a youth organisation for people between the ages of 12 and 18. The subjects range from Drill, Field Craft, First Aid, Shooting, Military Knowledge and Adventurous Training. In the ACF you learn self-discipline, teamwork, leadership, respect etc.

We received a lot of help from our local town, Nuneaton, and from the village of Atherstone, for which we are very grateful. ■

Royal Southern Yacht Club **Black Tie Event**

A group of Royal Southern Yacht Club members decided to organise a Black Tie Event for **Help for Heroes** in their wonderful waterside clubhouse on the Hamble River because they felt that they needed to raise money to help our returning war heroes who are in need of urgent help and support. ■

Our idea was to cycle non-stop, 24 hours a day, from the Army Training Centre 'ATC(P)' in Pirbright to Harwich, via Headley Court. Then to get the ferry to Esbjerg, Denmark, before cycling on through Denmark, Germany, the Netherlands, Belgium and into France, where we would rendezvous with 3 Para in Ranville, outside Caen, to celebrate the 65th Anniversary of the D-Day Landings, before continuing on to Le Havre, a ferry back to Portsmouth and return to ATC(P). The only stops would be for Headley Court, the ferry crossing and the D-Day celebrations.

The UK stage of the Ride went exactly to plan, with all legs being completed, not only on time but even faster than anticipated, with us reaching Harwich two hours ahead of schedule. The weather was fine, morale was high and everyone was looking forward to the task. However, only eight hours into the ferry crossing, we came across Force 7 winds and the brave few that attempted breakfast, quickly made a dive back to their beds as they saw waves actually going over the top of the ship!

Back on dry land, the rest of the route went pretty much to plan apart from Captain Kelly and myself – we went on to have four punctures and a split tyre between us! The team worked amazingly hard and we made it to Ranville by midday on the Saturday, very much looking forward to paying our respects and celebrating the 65th Anniversary. What we experienced that day in Caen will live with us for the rest of our lives: it was both humbling and awe-inspiring at the same time. How proud we felt. On Sunday we left for Le Havre and, luckily, had a quiet crossing this time. We arrived back into ATC(P) at around 2300hrs, exhausted, sore, but very happy at what we had achieved in aid of **Help for Heroes**. ∎

I joined the Royal Navy in 1998. I had previously been a professional rider, enjoyed mountain-biking and running marathons. I had been attracted to the Armed Forces by the promise of an active life, full of adventure and challenges. It never once occurred to me that my life could be changed so drastically during a simple training accident.

I don't remember much of the events of that day on the assault course. I fell from the 10ft wall and suffered an incomplete spinal cord injury, which eventually left me confined to a wheelchair.

Eventually, after trying unsuccessfully to overcome my injury, I was discharged from the Navy and gradually I became a recluse.

Months later, I met a guy in a wheelchair similar to mine, and he was accompanied by a Canine Partner. I'd never seen an 'Assistance Dog' before. These dogs can help their partners with dressing and undressing. They can open doors, press buttons and pick keys up off the floor. They can even empty the washing machine!

I was so excited I called Canine Partners immediately, and was invited to the two-week residential course. There are over 103 commands that a CP dog knows and I needed to learn them too. I was partnered with Lex, a boisterous but highly intelligent golden labrador. Within weeks, Lex and I were sailing around the Isle of Wight, wheeling across Exmoor and kayaking in Cumbria. Lex had given me the confidence to venture out and start enjoying life again.

I have even started riding again, and I have since become the UK's first Grade 1 Para-Equestrian show jumper. Should show jumping become a Paralympic sport I would love the chance to represent my country. Once again my life is filled with physical activity and sporting challenges, thanks largely to the support and confidence that Lex is able to give me.

If I hadn't had that chance meeting with the guy in the supermarket all those years ago, I would never have got Lex and I doubt very much if I would have got my life back to the extent that I have.

Of course, none of this would have been possible without Canine Partners, who raised Lex from a puppy and taught him all the amazing tasks. I am deeply grateful to them for giving Lex to me and for helping me to get my life back. ▓

Tarnia Venning-Heyhoe Help for Heroes **Festival at Newark Showground**

I am one of the lucky ones. My husband returned from Afghanistan fit and healthy. Throughout the months he was away I, like many, felt helpless and wanted to be able to do my bit for him and all the troops out in current conflict zones. The **Help for Heroes** Festival was born and it is my way of contributing to our heroes and showing **Help for Heroes** how grateful we are to them for supporting our troops and helping the injured get the best care they deserve. It was a great weekend. Everyone enjoyed themselves and we raised lots of well deserved funds for **Help for Heroes**. ▪

Armed Forces Day British Legion March, Greenford

'Greenford Royal British Legion and Greenford Royal Naval Association have been proud to support Help for Heroes since its inception as its work complements our own in caring for service and ex-service personnel.'

Don Macpherson

A battered £89 Renault Espace converted to Britain's first space shuttle, 5255 miles across Europe and Central Asia, travelling through the world's 16th most sparsely populated country, a desert, a dried up sea, various bars and hangovers, then, at the end, an England football match. And all for a good cause. Why **Help for Heroes**? Just our way of showing every serviceman and woman who has served or is serving how immensely proud we are of what they have, are and will continue to achieve.

The London–Tashkent Rally: despite the name, there's no racing or time trials involved, and neither were we starting from London or finishing in Tashkent; but then the Paris Dakar didn't always go from Paris–Dakar. The route we took saw us travel through France, Belgium, Holland, Germany, Poland, Ukraine, Russia, Kazakhstan and finally Kyrgyzstan. Along the way we visited Auschwitz, Kiev, Rostov, Volgagrad (formerly Stalingrad), a desert with really bad roads and the Aral Sea. We got arrested four times, had drugs planted on us at one border, saw the most amazing sights and met even more amazing locals.

The arrival date in Almaty was set to coincide with England playing Kazakhstan in a World Cup qualification game, and we had tickets waiting with our names on them! After amassing fifteen points from five games before the Kazakhstan game and comfortably heading their table, the chances were that England would sooner or later revert back to normal and lose points somewhere.

Luckily, this wasn't the case and a 4–0 thrashing left us in high spirits for the last leg of our little adventure. After the game, we made our way to Kyrgyzstan where the vehicles and contents were sold off locally and the money raised given to the local Voenno Antomovka Orphanage, Bishkek, where they care for children of all ages but in particular babies. ▪

Arklay Purdie, Dan Walker and Jamal Abbasi **The Jump for Heroes Project**

The Jump for Heroes Project was a skydive and cycle marathon, set up by university student and Parachute Regiment Reservist Arklay Purdie. Its aim was to raise money for **Help for Heroes**. Arklay took a break from his studies in 2008 to serve on Op HERRICK 8 with 2 PARA Patrols Platoon alongside L/Cpl Tom Neathway who was seriously injured by a booby trap. Seeing Tom stand to receive his medal from Prince Charles four months after the incident was motivation enough for Arklay to start the project. Arklay joined forces with fellow student Dan Walker and former Royal Marine Jamal Abbasi. Our project took the form of five sponsored tandem skydives. Starting on 6 June 2009 in John O' Groats, we cycled some 1300 miles to each event en route to Land's End, finishing on 15 July. We also visited a number of service institutions in order to share some of the media attention which we had attracted. We were welcomed warmly by Erskine Hospice, BLESMA, Selly Oak, Headley Court and the Parachute Regiment Association to name but

a few! We met some real characters along the way, including an Alzheimer's patient who was one of the first ever exponents of military parachuting. We received donations in parks, pubs, lay-bys, hostels and campsites. The overwhelming generosity of the public to support our efforts was staggering. We were humbled by their sheer enthusiasm to do their bit for those who have done theirs. One of our events occurred at a nightclub in Stourbridge which was attended by veterans from every British military campaign since the beginning of WW2, including Ben Parkinson, whose banter was on fire! In a few hours money was donated, as well as two mobility scooters, a PlayStation and a golf buggy! The only people who didn't throw money at us were the thousands of frustrated motorists whom we held up on the road! ∎

Pictured above: Arklay Purdie (blonde; cyclist), Jamal Abbasi (dark; cyclist), Dan Walker (ginger; support driver).

This page, clockwise from top left, Boris Johnson, Moira Stewart, Monty Don, Mark Foster, Michael Portillo, Nicholas Owen and Rhydian Roberts.

Opposite, clockwise from top left, Professor Robert Winston, Stephen Fry with Geoffrey Hughes, David Bellamy, Roddy Llewellyn, Rachel de Thame, Penny Mallory, Doug Richards and, centre, Saroj Chakravarty.

From left: Lance Corporal Farragher, Rifleman Turner,
Serjeant McAleese, Lance Corporal Shaw, and Rifleman Kirwan.

Subsequent to the inclusion of this photograph in *The Hero
Inside*, it is with great sadness that Serjeant Paul (Mac) McAleese
was killed in action on 20th August 2009 while going to the aid
of a wounded comrade. With 'a rucksack of talents' he was the
epitome of a true Royal Green Jacket and Rifleman.
One day his son, Charlie, will be able to read about his father
and be extremely proud.

Jake Curtin & Tim Andrew from The Art Group

'It's easy to forget how tough it is for these heroes when we are bombarded with imagery on the news, the action is a long way from home. Seeing Gill's portraits of the soldiers back on home soil brings the sacrifice being made daily into sharp focus. We are honoured to help in our small way, working with Gill to reproduce her imagery for the book and the framed pieces.'

Tom Newton Dunn, Defence Editor, The Sun

'The lengthy campaign that The Sun newspaper continues to run for **Help for Heroes** has been the most rewarding part of many of our journalistic careers.

The response we have had from our readers has been quite extraordinary, and has made us very proud of them. It has been a huge privilege to have played a small part in what can only be described as a national awakening.

Now, all of Britain appreciates Our Boys' and Girls' enduring sacrifice and courage. Long may that continue.'

Military Provost Guards Service, Corporal Dennis Merredew and Lance Corporal Paul Holmes

'We saw Gill who was a damsel in distress with a flat tyre and leapt to her rescue; the tyre was completely split!'

Sir Terry Leahy, Tesco's chief executive

'The men and women of the Armed Forces do a very difficult job which can mean that they and their families have to live with formidable consequences. On behalf of our staff and customers, Tesco is proud to support the **Help the Heroes** campaign.'